IS GOD A TRINITY?

Investigation into the biblical f
of the Trinity

CW01642126

That God is a Trinity has been Christian orthodoxy for over sixteen hundred years. According to the classical version of the doctrine God is three co-equal divine 'Persons' who have existed eternally together in a co-operative social relationship. Over the years Christians who have questioned it have been persecuted. Even today those Christians who reject the Trinity are treated as heretics.

This book argues that, despite its orthodoxy, the doctrine of the Trinity is unbiblical. There is no scriptural text that teaches the 'threeness' of God. The Trinitarian 'Persons', God the Father, God the Son and God the Spirit cannot be identified in scripture.

According to the Bible Jesus Christ is the begotten Son of God, not the incarnation of an 'Eternal Son'. Scriptural texts that appear to show a pre-existent 'Eternal Son' show nothing of the kind. Passages that are used to support a Trinity have better interpretations in terms of the one God who manifests himself as Word and Spirit.

David Kemball-Cook has a Cert H.E. in Theology from the Open Theological College, a Theological Studies Diploma, and a Religious Studies Certificate from Bible Way Training Institute. He has a first class degree in mathematics and philosophy from Oxford University and a doctorate in economics from London Business School.

Published by David Kemball-Cook

ISBN 10: 0-9542211-1-7

ISBN 13: 978-0-9542211-1-9

CONTENTS

1. THE DOCTRINE OF THE TRINITY

The Trinity is not a divine revelation

The Trinity is not a biblical doctrine

The Trinity has many problems and contradictions

Introduction

The doctrine that God is a Trinity has been orthodox Christian doctrine since the fourth century AD. According to the Trinity God is three co-equal divine 'Persons' who have existed in association together from eternity.

But how God can be three persons and still be one God? A common reply to this is to say ***'The Trinity is a divine mystery'***

However to say that the Trinity is a mystery is neither an explanation nor a justification for persecution. In previous centuries, non-trinitarians were executed[i]. Even nowadays, those Christians who question the Trinity are regarded by mainstream Christianity as denying the true God and being outside the faith[ii]. Sometimes it seems that more tolerance is shown to atheists and believers in other religions than to non-trinitarian Christians.

Although trinitarian ministers and writers teach that it is self-evident that God is a Trinity, the views of theologians can be quite different. Alister McGrath states that:

> The doctrine of the Trinity is unquestionably one of the most perplexing aspects of Christian theology[1]

Many theologians are quite openly sceptical. John Robinson, the New Testament scholar and Anglican bishop, wrote:

> Is there anyone whose heart does not sink a bit as Trinity Sunday comes round year by year? Certainly this must be true of preachers and I am sure it is true of most laymen. Just what is this of which we are supposed to make sense? 'The Father incomprehensible, the Son incomprehensible, the Holy Ghost incomprehensible' says the Athanasian Creed. 'The whole lot incomprehensible' says the ordinary man. How on earth have we got stuck with this abracadabra as the heart of the Christian faith? [2]

---

[1] A.E. McGrath, *Christian Theology: An Introduction*, p292.

[2] J.A.T. Robinson, *But that I can't believe!*, p86.

All Christians believe that God is revealed in Jesus Christ[iii].

But does this mean that Jesus Christ is the incarnation of an eternal divine person, a 'God the Son', who is a separate personality from another eternal divine person, 'God the Father'?

Christians believe that the Holy Spirit is God dwelling in the believer[iv].

But does this mean that there is a third divine person, a 'God the Spirit'?

In this book we shall examine the Trinity doctrine and the biblical evidence for it. We shall show not only that it is unbiblical but also that it has many problems and contradictions.

The classical doctrine of the Trinity

Chapter 2 describes the historical development of the Trinity doctrine. Briefly, the process that ended with a Trinity started from the belief that Jesus Christ was God, and yet that Jesus was different from God. So there were two objects of worship, Jesus and God, and yet only one God.

The theological attempts to account for this difficulty developed from the so-called 'Logos' (Greek for 'Word') doctrine in the second century AD. In Greek philosophy the Logos was thought to be a divine principle of the universe, subsidiary to a supreme God who was remote from creation, and a mediator between God and man. The Christian Apologists tried to bring together Greek philosophy and Christian theology by identifying this Logos with the Word that became flesh as Jesus Christ. The Logos then was called 'the Son' and thought to have a personal existence from eternity. The supreme God was then called 'the Father'. The result was two divine 'Persons', with 'the Father' the senior figure. From this 'binitarianism' developed the doctrine of the Trinity.

By the end of the 4th century AD the Trinity became the official doctrine of the Church. It is usually regarded as having been first proclaimed at the Council of Nicaea, the First Ecumenical Council, in AD 325. It is more accurate to date it from the Council of Constantinople, the Second Council, in AD 381, when the Holy Spirit was officially declared to be a 'Third Person' of equal rank to the other two 'Persons'.

The Trinity doctrine popularly taught today is essentially the same as in the original definitions, and can be termed the 'classical' Trinity. In the classical Trinity God consists of three eternally co-existing divine 'Persons'.

In the unity of the Godhead there be three persons, of one substance, power and eternity: God the Father, God the Son, and God the Holy Ghost (Westminster Confession, 1647)

The 'Persons' are known by different titles or names:

The First Person	***The Second Person***	***The Third Person***
God the Father	***God the Son***	***God the Spirit***
The Father	***The Son of God***	***God the Holy Ghost***
	The Son	***The Holy Spirit***
	The Eternal Son	***The Spirit***
	The Word of God	***The Spirit of God***
	Jesus Christ	

<u>The classical Trinity</u>

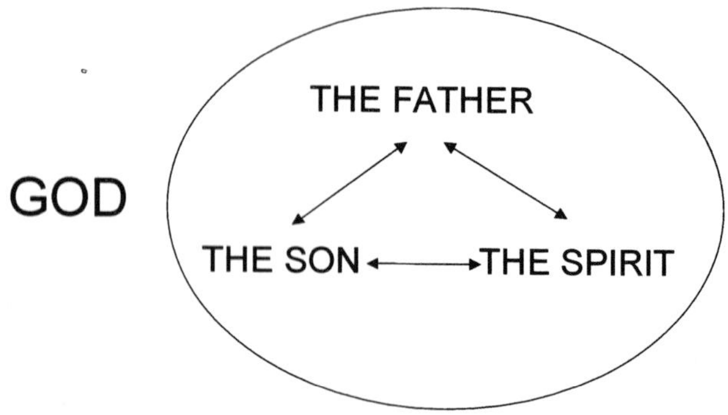

According to the classical Trinity, the three 'Persons' have equal status ('co-equal'), have existed together since before the creation of the world ('co-eternal') and have the same essence or nature ('consubstantial'). The 'Persons' have their own personalities and centres of consciousness. The Trinity is an *eternal society* in which the Persons associate and make agreements with each other.

The Trinity doctrine claims to be able to explain the Incarnation by 'God the Son' coming down to earth and took human form as Jesus Christ. When he did so, he left behind his heavenly glory and voluntarily gave up use of his divine powers. Jesus is a 'God-man', with two natures, divine and human, but only one personality.

The Incarnation according to the classical Trinity.

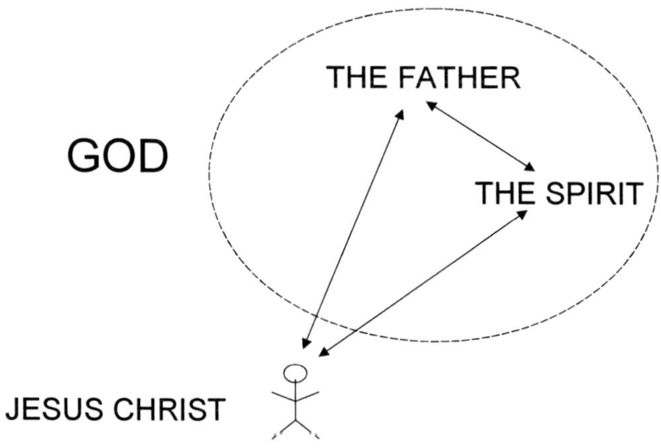

There were three 'Persons' in heaven before the Incarnation. When the Son came to earth he left behind two Persons. When he went back to heaven, there were three Persons again before the Holy Spirit left to dwell in believers.

The 'Persons' of the Trinity are supposed to be of equal status. However in practical terms 'God the Father' is the senior figure. When Christians pray, they pray 'to the Father through the Son' (John 16:23). 'God the Son' and 'God the Spirit' are then seen as *intermediaries* between the believer and 'God the Father'. A natural question is whether, if 'God the Father' is the 'Person' that Christians pray to, God the Father is the only real God and the other two Persons are some kind of second-rank divine beings not fully God? 'God the Father' is frequently confused with 'God' himself

Given that the doctrine of the Trinity is supposedly a fundamental doctrine of Christianity, it should be of great importance to teach it correctly. Most Christians are familiar with references to the Trinity and know that it is supposedly fundamental to their faith. But how many times have Christians heard or read a straightforward exposition of the doctrine in terms accessible to the layman? Often the Trinity is referred to in passing, perhaps with a reference to 'Let *us* make man' (Genesis 1:26), but it is rarely the central theme of teaching.

What practical difference does the Trinity make to the 'ordinary' Christian today? The theologian Karl Rahner has noted that:

> Despite their orthodox confession of the Trinity, Christians are, in their practical life, almost mere monotheists. We must be willing to admit that, should the doctrine of the Trinity be dropped as false, the major part of religious literature could well remain virtually unchanged.[3]

In other words, the doctrine of the Trinity makes no practical difference to many Christians, who address God as 'Thou' and not as a plurality of three. The confusion and false image of Christianity that it has brought are discussed later[4].

Some main problems with the Trinity

The classical Trinity involves many problems, confusions and contradictions. Here are some of the main problems, with some brief notes and references to where they are discussed more fully later.

The Bible does not show God as three Persons

Trinitarians seek to find a Trinity in the Old Testament by citing plural pronouns used for God and manifestations suggesting plurality. In particular there is heavy reliance on 'Let *us* make man' (Genesis 1:26). However use of plural pronouns referring to God is rare, is in any case explicable by the 'plural of majesty' and is vastly outnumbered by the thousands of singular pronouns and the emphasis upon the singularity of God.

The doctrine of the Trinity is not stated explicitly anywhere in the New Testament[v]. There is no mention for instance of 'the threeness' of God in any of Paul's doctrinal epistles. The terms 'God the Son' and 'God the Holy Spirit' are not biblical terms. The term 'God the Father' is found in the New Testament (for instance in Paul's salutations); but when it is used it is as a synonym for God in his entirety, an abbreviation for 'God the Father of our Lord Jesus Christ'. 'God the Father' is never used in the trinitarian sense. The

---

[3] K. Rahner, *The Trinity*, p10.

[4] See Chapter 7.

Holy Spirit, although clearly a personal manifestation of God, has no personality of its (or his) own, separate from that of God.

Texts that supposedly show a Trinity are outnumbered by far by texts in which God (or 'the Father') and Jesus Christ (or 'the Son') are described together *without any reference to the Spirit.* Such texts, with God and Jesus mentioned in the same context, occur in the hundreds throughout the epistles and the Book of Revelation. For instance consider the salutations in the epistles from (e.g.) 'God our Father and the Lord Jesus Christ'. Not a single salutation is from the Holy Spirit as well.

There is no scriptural evidence for three Persons in heaven. Trinitarians give different answers to the question of how many Persons are in heaven now, or how many the believer will be able to see when he goes to heaven. Some trinitarians say one, some say three, and some say three *and* one. No texts describe three in heaven, while numerous texts mention *two.* As with the salutations, the two are God and Christ, not the First and Second Persons of a Trinity, and there is no mention of a Third Person. Consider for example Revelation 4-5. There is one seated on the throne and there is the Lamb standing before the throne, but there is no sign of the Spirit except in the form of seven torches 'which are the seven spirits of God'. If God were a Trinity, one would expect to see something more of the 'Third Person' in this scene.

In fact, the New Testament gives consistent witness to the risen Christ at the right hand of God in heaven, but *never* to a 'Second Person' at the right hand of a 'First Person', and *never* describes a 'Third Person' anywhere in spatial relation to the two.

See Chapters 3, 4, 5 and 6

The Trinity doctrine uses 'Person' inconsistently

According to the Trinity, God is three 'Persons'. Much depends on what is meant by 'person'. It is here that the doctrine has a major weakness. Is a 'person' of the Trinity a 'person' something like a human 'person', meaning a separate personality with its own will, memories, emotions and voice? Or does 'person', when applied to God, mean just a personal way in which God manifests himself?

We might call the former idea of 'person' a 'strong' definition, and the latter idea a 'weak' definition. The two meanings are quite different, but are often confused. The confusion over the meaning of 'person' goes back to the original definitions used when the Trinity was formulated, and is partly due to the different languages used. In the Western Roman Empire, the Latin word *persona* was used. This means something like a 'mask' or a 'role', and close to the weak sense of 'person'. In the East, the Greek word *hypostasis* was used, meaning something like 'independent existence' and is clearly much closer to the strong sense of 'person'. The difference in meanings of the terms used was a frequent source of confusion and misunderstanding.

God may be three (or more) 'persons' in the weak sense without being three 'persons' in the strong sense. For instance God may manifest himself as his Word, but that does not imply that the Word is a separate personality within the Godhead. God may manifest himself as Spirit, but that does not mean that the Spirit is a separate personality from some other person 'the Father'.

The classical Trinity needs the strong definition of 'person'. The reason is quite simple: the doctrine of the Trinity supposedly explains the fact that Jesus had a separate personality *in the 'strong' sense* from that of 'the Father'. Jesus clearly had both a different will and a different memory from the God he called 'Father'. When Jesus said in Gethsemane:

Not my will, but thine be done (Luke 22:42)

he was subordinating his will to God's will. This would be nonsense if Jesus and God had the same will[vi]. The classical Trinity interprets this, as all Jesus' prayers, as the 'God the Son' talking to the 'God the Father'. When Jesus said:

Glorify thou me … with the glory which I had with thee before the world was (John 17:5)

the trinitarian interpretation is that Jesus is talking with the consciousness and memory of the 'Eternal Son' about the time he remembers with 'the Father' before the creation of the world.

Therefore if there is a 'God the Son' who became incarnate as Jesus, this 'God the Son' has to be a different 'person' in the *strong* sense from the 'God the Father'.

The view that the 'Persons' of the Trinity are different 'persons' in the strong sense presents real difficulties. The critic asks, quite reasonably:

Are not these 'Persons' really different beings, and so three Gods?

Three different 'Persons' in the strong sense is dangerously close to three gods, tritheism.

Geoffrey Lampe, in the Bampton Lectures 1976, makes this point:

> One effect of (the adoption of the concept of the pre-existent Son as the model for Christology) was to make it seem plausible to give to the term 'person' ... the full meaning which it received in Boethius' definition: 'an individual substance of a rational nature'. The Christian concept of God then becomes inescapably tritheistic; for three 'persons' in anything like the modern sense of the word 'person' mean in fact three Gods. Yet when the Second Person is conceived of as Jesus Christ, 'person' can scarcely be understood in any other sense than this.[5]

Trinitarian argument tends to confuse the two senses of 'person' in order to avoid the accusation of tritheism. It is normal and scriptural to talk about God manifesting Himself in different roles, showing various attributes, manifesting Himself in different ways and so on. The trinitarian method of argument is to use this fact that God exists as more than one 'person' in the weak sense to conclude that God exists as three 'persons' in the strong sense. This inconsistency in the definition of 'person' has never been acknowledged in trinitarian argument.

There are other difficulties associated with the idea that God is three 'Persons'. Firstly, how many Persons indwell the believer? Are there three, two or one? The three persons of the Trinity are supposed to be inseparable, in the sense that we can never speak about one of them being present while the others are absent. Trinitarians give different answers to this question. Some say just one person is in the believer. Others claim to be able to distinguish all three, but without any real scriptural foundation for their view.

See Chapters 2, 4 and 5

Trinitarian argument often assumes what it tries to prove

It often seems that trinitarian argument assumes what it is trying to prove. For example, a typical argument commences with the assumptions of the three 'Persons': 'God the Father', 'God the Son' and 'God the Spirit'. They are *assumed* a) to exist and b) to be the same kind of 'person'. The next move is to try to establish that the three are *different* persons. In the John Ankerberg debate[6] between trinitarians and representatives of the United Pentecostal Church, the trinitarian scholar Walter Martin did exactly that. He said:

---

[5] G. Lampe, *God as Spirit*, pp135f.

[6] The John Ankerberg debate between trinitarian scholars and representatives of the United Pentecostal Congress, John Ankerberg et al, 1985.

"We agree that the Father is God, the Son is God and that the Spirit is God. We only differ about whether they are distinct persons."

To take another example, the trinitarian scholar R.M. Bowman, in *The Biblical Basis of the Doctrine of the Trinity*[7], has a heading 'The Father, the Son and the Spirit are distinct persons'. Under this heading Bowman has subheadings 'God the Father and the Son Jesus Christ are two persons' and 'Jesus is not God the Father' under which he lists texts which appear to support those propositions. Bowman makes the assumption that he is trying to prove.

It is incorrect to start talking about 'the Father', 'the Son' and 'the Spirit' as if they were the same kind of being or person, and then to try to prove that they are different persons. In fact, the Bible does not refer to any such person as 'the Father' who is different from God Himself. It cannot be taken for granted that the terms 'The Son' and 'the Spirit' refer to persons with the same kind of existence as 'the Father'. To use the terms ' the Father', 'The Son' and 'The Spirit' does not imply that they refer to 'persons' with the same kind of existence as each other.

See Chapters 4, 5 and 6

A 'God the Son' means two gods

The Trinity needs different 'Persons' in the 'strong' sense of different personalities. But if the 'God the Son' has a different will from 'God the Father', then it would seem that God has two wills. The contradictions have never been resolved[vii]. So either God has two wills or there are two gods.

See Chapters 2 and 5

An 'Eternal Son' cannot be begotten

The notion of an Eternal Son cannot be reconciled with the biblical truth that Jesus is the begotten Son of God, and so that the Sonship began at a moment in history.

See Chapters 2 and 5

---

[7] R.M. Bowman, *The Biblical Basis of the Doctrine of the Trinity*, pp10-11.

A 'God the Son' cannot pray to a 'God the Father'

Jesus prays to 'the Father' and talks about 'my Father in heaven' as God. A Second Person of a Trinity could never address a First Person as God or pray to him. Only a *man* can do that.

A trinitarian reply would say that Jesus can pray genuinely to the Father because he is man as well as God. The trinitarian idea of Jesus as a 'God-man' needs Jesus to have the personality of the pre-existent 'God the Son', and this would violate his humanity. Jesus cannot be an authentic human being and also have (sometimes) the voice and memory of an 'Eternal Son'.

See Chapter 5

A 'God the Son' cannot mediate between God and man

A 'God the Son' cannot mediate between God and man, or between a 'God the Father' and man[8]. Again, the trinitarian reply would rest on the 'God-man' idea of Jesus. Because Jesus is both God and man, *as man*, he can be the mediator and the sacrifice for sin[9]. However Jesus cannot be a 'God-man' in the sense that is needed for the Trinity because such a 'God-man' would not be an authentic human being.

See Chapter 5

Non-trinitarian views

The three faiths claiming descent from Abraham, Judaism, Christianity and Islam, all agree there is only one God (the principle of monotheism). However orthodox Christianity differs from Islam and Judaism over whether the one God is *singular* or *plural* in nature.

Most Jews[viii] do not see God represented as three persons in the Old Testament and see the Trinity as a violation of the essentially singular nature of God. The Jewish understanding of God is expressed in the *Shema*

The Lord our God is one Lord (Deuteronomy 6:4)[ix]

---

[8] Trinitarian language often confuses the triune God with 'God the Father'

[9] See e.g. 1 Timothy 2:5f, Hebrews 9:12-15.

Islam also rejects the Trinity[x]. A central doctrine in Islam is the *tawhid*, the oneness of God. It is an important part of Islamic differentiation between what it sees as the true religion of the Book, Islam, and the corruption of the true doctrine that it sees in Christianity. The Qur'anic rebuttal of the trinitarian idea that God is three Persons in one is to be found in Sura 4:

The Messiah, Jesus son of Mary, was only the Messenger of God, and His Word that He committed to Mary, and a Spirit from Him. So believe in God and His Messengers, and say not 'Three'. Refrain; better is it for you. God is only one God (Sura 4:168)

Turning to alternative views that describe themselves as Christian, there are three fundamental beliefs that are relevant:

- **God is one**
- **Jesus Christ is God**
- **There is a distinction between God and Jesus**

There are problems in believing all three to be true at the same time. If God is one, and God is different from Jesus, how can Jesus be God? If Jesus is God, how can he be different from God? If Jesus is God, and different from God, how can God be one?

The first principle that God is one has been taken to mean both *monotheism*, meaning that there is only one God, and also *singularity*, meaning that the one God is a unity in his being. Monotheism is, of course, emphasized in the Old Testament (see e.g. Deuteronomy 6:4, Isaiah 44:6), and confirmed by Jesus (see Mark 12:29). There are no other gods beside the one true God. *Singularity* is a different matter. Trinitarians would say that God is one God, but three 'Persons', and that the 'threeness' of God is confirmed in the Bible.

There is often confusion between these two meanings. Consider for instance the following possible dialogue between a trinitarian and a non-trinitarian:

Trinitarian: *"I believe that God is one"*

Non-trinitarian: *"You do not believe that God is one, you believe that God is three"*

Trinitarian: *"I believe that God is one and three"*

Non-trinitarian: *"You are contradicting yourself!"*

Trinitarians are not contradicting themselves when they say that God is both one *and* three, because they believe there is only one God, but he is plural in nature. This can be easily misunderstood by non-trinitarians.

The second principle is the Incarnation, that Jesus Christ is God in the flesh. Christ is described sometimes as the 'God-man', fully man and fully God.

The third principle is the distinction between God and Jesus. It is clear from the gospels that there must be some difference between Jesus and God, and there is a *relationship* between them. Jesus talks about God as other than himself, greater than himself and so on. He prayed to God, and he prayed even when there was nobody around to see him (e.g. Luke 6:12, 22:41-45). Unless we are to believe that Jesus' talk about God as other than himself was untruth, and that his prayer was not just a pretence, then we have to accept a distinction in personality between Jesus and the God whom he called 'the Father'.

Historically, different theological positions come from emphasizing *two* of the beliefs at the expense of the third. Here is a brief summary (see Chapter 2 for a more complete account).

Binitarianism and trinitarianism emphasized the second and third beliefs at the risk of violating monotheism. Modalism (believing that Father, Son and Spirit are modes or appearances of the one God) emphasized the first and the second beliefs at the risk of the distinction between God and Jesus. Adoptionism and later dynamic monarchianism (holding that Christ was only human) and Arianism (believing Christ was a created being) emphasized the first and the third beliefs at the expense of the full deity of Christ.

In the debates of the third and fourth centuries the trinitarian position developed in the course of conflict with modalism and then with Arianism. The final formulation was adopted by the Council of Constantinople in AD 381. Positions like Arianism that denied the full divinity of Christ were condemned as heresy. Likewise modalist positions that appeared to threaten the Father-Son distinction were labelled as Sabellian and condemned, but not before long running and bitter debates. Fear of Sabellianism has remained a constant factor in Catholic theology ever since. Believers who have denied the Trinity have been classed as heretics, and often persecuted, by the orthodox church. There is considerable hostility today from trinitarian orthodoxy towards those who question or deny the Trinity[xi].

After the Reformation of the sixteenth century, the Trinity doctrine was taken over without question by the Lutheran and Protestant organisations. However individuals and groups denying the Trinity, known as unitarian or Socinian, appeared at this time.

There are at least three main strands of modern non-trinitarianism. The first is ***oneness pentecostalism***. This grew out of the pentecostal revival of the early twentieth century[xii]. The emphasis in oneness pentecostal doctrine is on the revealed name of God as Jesus and baptism in the name of Jesus only. It follows the modalism of the second century regarding Christ as a manifestation of the one God, but shares the belief of trinitarians that Jesus is a 'God-man', both God and man. However Christ is seen as God himself incarnate rather than a 'God the Son' incarnate. Oneness pentecostalism maintains strongly both the unity of God and the deity of Christ. A challenge for this view is to adequately account for the distinction between Father and Son; this is described by a leading oneness pentecostal theologian as the distinction between the one God in his transcendence and the one God as he is manifested in flesh[10].

The second type of non-trinitarian view is ***biblical unitarianism***. This follows dynamic monarchianism in emphasizing the oneness of God and the humanity of Christ. Christ's displays of divine power are seen as coming from the anointing of the indwelling Spirit rather than a divine nature. Biblical unitarianism maintains the unity of God and the distinction between Father and Son, but denies the deity of Christ[11]. A challenge for unitarian views is to explain the many biblical texts commonly cited to show the deity of Christ.

The third type of non-trinitarian belief follows the general line of the Arian thought of the fourth century in viewing ***Jesus as a pre-existent but created being***. This view maintains the unity of God and the distinction between Father and Son, but at the expense of the deity of the incarnate Christ. This kind of view is expressed by, for instance, Associated Bible Students[12], who maintain that Jesus was a spirit being who became a genuine man and was raised to divine status at resurrection. A challenge for this view is to maintain the integrity and humanity of Christ's personality in the face of his pre-existent nature.

---

[10] See D. Bernard, *The Oneness of God*, pp121f, 127.

[11] See Graeser, Lynn and Schoenheit, *One God, One Lord*, 2003.

[12] *The Doctrine of Christ* by Associated Bible Students.

The table shows how trinitarianism and these alternatives relate to the three beliefs about God and Christ. 'Yes' to a principle from a certain view means that the principle is clearly satisfied by that view. 'Claims Yes' indicates this author's view that there are difficulties with the claim[xiii].

PRINCIPLE	TRINITY	ONENESS PENTECOSTAL / MODALISM	ADOPTIONISM / UNITARIANISM	ARIANISM
1. Monotheism	Claims Yes	Yes	Yes	Yes
2. Deity of Jesus Christ	Claims Yes	Yes	Denies deity of Christ	Denies full deity of Christ
3. Father-Son distinction	Claims Yes	Claims Yes	Yes	Yes

It is not the purpose of this book to contend for any of the Christian non-trinitarian alternatives described here, but rather to show the inadequacy of the classical Trinity. The doctrine of the Trinity claims to satisfy monotheism, guarantee the deity of Christ and to account for the relationship between Jesus and God. In fact it fails in all three areas.

The rest of this book

We have highlighted some of the problems of the classical Trinity to be discussed in detail in the following chapters.

Some problems of the doctrine of the classical Trinity

- **The Bible does not describe God as three 'Persons'**
- **The Trinity defines 'Person' inconsistently**
- **Trinitarian argument often assumes what it attempts to prove**
- **A 'God the Son' means two gods**
- **An 'Eternal Son' cannot be begotten**
- **A 'God the Son' cannot pray to a 'God the Father'**
- **A 'God the Son' cannot be a mediator between God and man**

Chapter 2 gives a historical survey of the development of the doctrine of the Trinity. Chapter 3 outlines the biblical evidence used to support the doctrine, and shows that it does not show a Trinity. The Trinity doctrine itself and the trinitarian 'Persons' cannot be found anywhere in the Bible. Chapters 4, 5 and 6 focus on the doctrines of the 'God the Father', 'God the Son' and 'God the Spirit' respectively.

Chapter 7 summarizes the failures of trinitarian doctrine and discusses how the one God may be understood as showing himself in different personal ways without being a Trinity.

2. HISTORICAL SURVEY

The Trinity doctrine was not known to the first century Church

The fourth century 'classical' Trinity was significantly influenced by pagan ideas and philosophy

Modern theologians have tried to reinterpret the Trinity doctrine

Introduction

Trinitarians often claim that:

1. *The doctrine of the Trinity was held by the Church consistently and without variation from the first century until the present day.*

2. *Objections to the Trinity are quite recent and historically unimportant*

3. *The Trinity doctrine has been accepted by the vast majority of Christians down the ages.*

All of these claims are false. There can be considerable doubt as to whether the first century church had a belief in God as a Trinity at all. Certainly the epistles of Paul contain no clear statement of the doctrine.

In fact it took over three hundred years before the Trinity doctrine arrived in its present form. It was not until the late fourth century AD that the Holy Spirit was admitted to full status as the 'Third Person'. Early formulations were 'binitarian', admitting only two divine entities, a supreme God ('the Father') and the Word ('the Son'). Before the fourth century, all the formulations were 'subordinationist', with 'the Father' quite clearly the first in importance and the source of the other two. Some formulations were blatantly tritheistic, amounting to belief in three distinct gods.

Doctrinal development was not smooth but was characterized by controversies and bitter divisions. Some remain to this day, such as the difference between East and West over the *filioque* clause in Western creeds. Modern theology has shown that the contradictions and problems of the fourth century definitions have not disappeared. Many twentieth century theologians have revised, re-interpreted or simply rejected the classical Trinity.

The Apostolic Church (1st century AD)

The church in the first century AD is described as the Apostolic Church, for the obvious reason that it was under the leadership of the apostles, mainly Paul, Peter and John, and their immediate successors. It is clear from the New Testament that the Apostolic Church believed Jesus Christ was fully human but also an object of worship[xiv].

The Apostolic Church was also firmly monotheistic, inheriting the belief of the Jews in one God. It therefore seems that the Church was able to reconcile monotheism with having two objects of worship, Jesus and God. There is no evidence that any of the Jewish apostles (Paul, Peter, John) saw a conflict between Christianity and monotheism. However, even if the Church saw no conflict at the time between monotheism and two objects of worship, later generations would ask the question:

How could there be one God, and Jesus Christ be God also?

The trinitarian answer to this question is examined in Chapter 5.

Did the Apostolic Church believe in a Trinity? Trinitarians will say yes, and cite the New Testament as proof. Although neither the term nor an explicit statement of the Trinity doctrine can be found in scripture, a trinitarian would say that the New Testament, viewed as a whole, depicts a God who demands to be understood in a trinitarian way. However this is to look at the New Testament through trinitarian spectacles. If the Apostle Paul, say, were alive today, would he say that his writings show God is a Trinity? Would he have even understood trinitarian concepts? Consider for example this greeting:

Grace be to you, and peace from God the Father, and from our Lord Jesus Christ

(Galatians 1:3)

A trinitarian would understand it as a greeting from the First and Second Persons. However it seems very unlikely that Paul was thinking in those terms when he wrote it. The problem of finding the trinitarian 'God the Father' in the New Testament is examined in Chapter 4.

In conclusion, the Apostolic Church reconciled belief in one God with worship of both God and the Lord Jesus Christ. But this does not prove that the Apostolic Church believed in a Trinity.

The post-apostolic church (90-140AD)

The period following the Apostolic Church is sometimes known as that of the Apostolic Fathers. They include Clement of Rome (perhaps the same Clement as the Bishop of Rome at that time), Ignatius (Bishop of Antioch), Polycarp (Bishop of Smyrna), Papias, Hermas and the anonymous author(s) of the *Didache*. They are termed 'apostolic' because it is believed that they either knew or derived their teaching from the apostles. Therefore this period is an important one when considering questions of doctrine.

David Bernard, in *Oneness and Trinity, AD 100-300*, analyses ancient Christian writings to try to determine the extent to which the early church can be said to be trinitarian. There are two questions:

1. *Whether it was believed that God was one person, as opposed to three persons*
2. *Whether it was believed that Jesus Christ was God*

Bernard believes that there is good evidence that some at least of the Apostolic Fathers would not dissent from the non-trinitarian, or 'oneness', belief that God is one and not three. He suggests that passages in their writings that suggest a trinitarian position may be either:

(a) elaborations of New Testament passages which are capable of being interpreted in a oneness light (for instance Matthew 28:19); or

(b) later additions, alterations or interpolations (for instance from the fourth century).

In *I Clement*, Clement writes from Rome to Corinth (to urge the Corinthians to think again, after they had deposed their leaders). Bernard identifies the emphasis that Clement places upon the singular name of God. He notes that only two sentences could be seen to imply a Trinity. One of these is reminiscent of Ephesians 4:4-6, where the key thought is the three ways in which God can be known, and does not imply the classical Trinity. The other passage exists only in one Greek manuscript (dated AD 1056) and is missing from the other one.

Ignatius, Bishop of Antioch (martyred c AD 115) is known for his passionate emphasis upon the divinity of Christ. He stated that 'Christ was truly God' and spoke about 'Jesus Christ our God', 'the Blood of God', 'God existing in flesh'. He also wrote of God being manifested in human form, and 'There is one God, who has manifested himself by Jesus Christ his Son, who is his eternal Word'.

Bernard points out[13] that along with 7 genuine letters of Ignatius there are 6 spurious ones dating from the fourth century and 3 from the twelfth century, and that there are passages in the spurious ones that attempt to credit him with trinitarian sayings. Furthermore there are long versions of his letters which appear to be filled with fourth century interpolations, some of which add trinitarian-sounding glosses to the original ('medium') version. Trinitarian-sounding passsages in his (genuine) letters can be accounted for as parallel to New Testament scriptures such as 2 Corinthian 13:14 or John 1:1[14]. The study of Ignatius indicates that:

1. *Ignatius would, if faced with a choice, declare for non-trinitarian belief.*

2. *Later writers were keen to disguise Ignatius' true beliefs and to portray him as a trinitarian.*

The *Didache* is particularly relevant because it contains the first so-called trinitarian formula for baptism outside the New Testament, using the words of Matthew 28:19

'... *to baptise into the name of the Father, and of Son, and of the Holy Spirit'*

Some trinitarian scholars have claimed[15] that the *Didache* is as early as AD 35-60, and therefore predates some New Testament writings. If true, this would give support to the view that the apostolic church was trinitarian in belief. However most scholars place the *Didache* in the period AD 70-110[16]. Bernard quotes[17] other studies which question the reliability of the document as a guide to apostolic beliefs and practices, mentioning the likelihood of changes in the 900 years between its date of writing and the only surviving copy dated 1056, and also the mention of practices (such as fasting before baptism) which are not biblical. The prayers are addressed to the Father, not to the Father, Son and Holy Spirit. In any case, the use of a baptismal formula based on Matthew 28:19 is not conclusive for trinitarian belief for this period.[18] The *Didache* itself (Bernard notes) also refers to baptism into the name (singular) of the Lord, and the same passage refers to the Lord as Jesus.

---

13 Bernard, *Oneness and Trinity*, pp37f.

14 See Chapters 3 and 4 for discussion of 2 Corinthians 13:14 and John 1:1 respectively.

15 Bernard in *Oneness and Trinity*, p48, quotes E. Calvin Beisner making this assertion in 1988.

16 See e.g. Henry Chadwick, *The Early Church*, p47.

17 Bernard, *Oneness and Trinity*, pp46-55.

18 See Chapter 3 for discussion of the significance of Matthew 28:19.

Gnosticism (c AD 100-200)

The varieties of belief known as gnosticism arose in the second century. Generally speaking, gnosticism was a mixture of Eastern religion with Christianity. The term itself arises from *gnosis*, the Greek word for knowledge, and a common theme is secret knowledge known only to an elite of 'superbelievers'. Only to the elite was salvation guaranteed, but sometimes the 'ordinary believer' had a chance. There were more than a dozen different schools. However almost all of them were *dualist*, believing that spirit was 'good' and matter 'bad', and that redemption consisted of an ascent of the soul from the 'bad' material sphere to the 'spirit' realm. The Saviour could not therefore be material, and the creator of the material world could not be a good god.

Hence gnosticism tended to cluster around two beliefs about God and Jesus

1. The supreme God (spirit) was superior to another god who created the material world. Often the latter was the Old Testament Yahweh (Marcion for instance believed this).

2. Docetism - Jesus was not human, but some angelic creation of the supreme God.

The post-apostolic church fought the gnostic heresies with three main weapons

a) The claim of apostolic succession for the main churches, whereby leadership was handed down in an unbroken chain from the apostles to (their) present day. This would rule out the idea that the apostles held to gnostic doctrine.

b) The idea of the Church as the Body of Christ, unified and in agreement, contrasting with the differing, and disagreeing, gnostic schools.

c) The determination of which texts were to be recognised as authoritative scripture[xv]*.*

The battle was exemplified in the work of Irenaeus, Bishop of Lyons. By about AD 200 the canon of scripture had been almost completely established, and the gnostic texts excluded. However disagreements over the nature of the Godhead were to continue.

Pagan influence upon Christian doctrine

Adolf von Harnack, in his *History of Dogma*[19], commented that the development of Christian doctrine in the 2nd and 3rd centuries AD was influenced heavily by

[19] Adolf von Harnack, *History of Dogma* (1886-9), summarised in McGrath *Christian Theology: An Introduction*, pp311 3.

the Greek-speaking, termed 'Hellenistic', culture of the time. As a result Christian doctrine was removed from its roots in primitive Christianity and Hebrew modes of thought, and became much an exercise in abstract thought and speculative metaphysics. In the case of the doctrine of the Person of Christ, Harnack focuses his attention particularly upon gnosticism, the 'Logos-Christology' of the Apologists and trinitarian theologians.

More specifically, during the 2nd century Christian thinkers were subject to influence from what is known as Middle Platonism, a philosophical movement deriving from the Greek philosopher Plato of the 5th century BC. James J. Heaney, in *A New Dictionary of Christian Theology* notes that the most important contributions of Middle Platonism to the Christian doctrine of God were:

1. *Replacement of the Creator of Genesis 2 who was personally involved with his creation by an abstract, remote and unknowable figure, a 'Supreme God', source of all.*

2. *A theology of 'emanation' to describe beings coming out from the Supreme God who mediate between the supreme God and creation and perform essential tasks. For pagan Platonists these were either the Platonic Ideas or a lesser race of 'daemons'.*[20]

For the Christian theologians under Platonic influence such as Justin, Irenaeus, Tertullian, Clement and Origen, these mediating beings were the *Logos* (Greek for Word) and the Spirit. The Platonic idea of 'emanation' corresponds in Christian terms to so-called 'economic' activity, whereby a divine figure performs specific functions within the divine order. Thus, an 'economic' function of the Logos is to mediate truth, and a function of the Spirit is to give divine inspiration.

J.P.Mackey in the *New Dictionary of Christian Theology* argues that the inevitable result of applying Greek theology to the Christian doctrine of God is *subordinationism.* The mediating Logos and Spirit, because they must be 'persons', they must be 'lower than', subordinate to, the One Supreme God:

> Since the Greek model is unalterably 'economic' (i.e. designed specifically to find names for God (Word, Spirit) which related to the creation of the world and God's action within it) ... those who appropriate it to describe really distinct levels or grades or 'persons' within the divinity cannot avoid the implication that these are successively 'lower than', subordinate to the One God, unoriginate source of all. The only way to avoid this implication would be to replace the model[21]

---

[20] James J. Heaney, Middle Platonism, *A New Dictionary of Christian Theology*, p368.

[21] J. P. Mackey, Doctrine of the Trinity, *A New Dictionary of Christian Theology*, p583.

As well as the general Platonic influence on theology, beliefs in a divine trinity were common in pagan thought of the second to fourth centuries. The classicist and Egyptologist J. Gwyn Griffiths, in *Triads and Trinity*, examined the pagan roots of a threefold idea of God. He noted that in Egypt the concept of God as trinity or triad was of ancient origin, with the best known example being Osiris, Isis and Horus (father, mother, child), but that it was flourishing in the 2nd century and afterwards, particularly in Alexandria. During this time it took the form of a mystery cult of Isis. The Alexandrian theologians Clement and Origen could have been influenced by their contact with and familiarity with these Egyptian triadic traditions

From the 3rd to the 6th centuries the neoplatonist philosophical school[xvi] continued the Platonic philosophical tradition. Plotinus (c205-270), one of the founders of neoplatonism, postulated three cosmic principles:

1. *The One or the Good, the supreme cause of all things*
2. *The Nous (reason), the image of the One*
3. *The Psyche (soul), which mediates between the Nous and the material world*

There is a suggestive, but clear, parallel[xvii] of the neoplatonic trinity with the doctrine of the Christian Trinity that was being developed at the same time[22]. Although it would be wrong to claim that the Trinity is pagan in origin, it is quite possible that the pagan triadic ideas influenced the early Christian trinitarians, even if only subconsciously.

The Apologists and the Logos theology (AD 130-180)

The Christian Apologists of the second century attempted to justify Christianity to non-Christians, using concepts and figures from pagan thought. Justin, known as Martyr, was the most important. Other Apologists were Justins'disciple Tatian, Aristides, Theophilus Bishop of Antioch and Athenagoras of Athens. They were mainly philosophers not churchmen. Their methods involved

1. *The introduction of a subordinationism between a supreme God and a second God.*

---

[22] It is recorded that Plotinus' teacher Ammonius Saccas had another pupil named Origen, who may have been the trinitarian theologian Origen.

2. The elevation of philosophy and cosmology above scripture.

Justin saw continuity in the action of God between Jew and Gentile through the ages, working through Old Testament saints and pagan philosophers alike to witness to Himself and prepare the world for Christ. Abraham and Socrates were both 'Christians before Christ'. All human history and philosophy leads to Christ. Following the line of Paul's sermon in Athens recorded in Acts 17, the Apologists held that God implanted seeds of truth in many places in order that man might seek after him and know him.

For the Apologists therefore, pagan philosophy contains much truth. Not only the mind, but also the heart, bear witness to God. The Apologists developed the statements made by Paul in Roman 1 along the lines that God has implanted in all men a moral sense or conscience, so that even pagans may know what is right and what is wrong.

The so-called 'Logos theology' comes from the attempts by the Apologists to use the contemporary non-Christian concepts of 'Logos' to interpret the use of the term in the Prologue to the Gospel of John, where Christ is described as the Word made flesh. The divine Logos was a common philosophical idea of the time, being significant in both Platonism and Stoicism. For Platonism, the Logos was an intermediary between a remote supreme God and creation. For Stoicism, the Logos was the rational principle of the universe. Edward Hardy, translator of Justin's work, describes the Logos as 'floating in the air of popular Greek philosophy and Hellenistic Judaism ... the word 'logos' (means) everything except a single word - speech, design, argument, reason - therefore God's thought, plan, utterance and so on'[23].

Before Justin, connections had already been made between the Logos and the God of the Bible. The Jewish Greek-speaking philosopher Philo of Alexandria, living at the time of Christ, had identified the Logos as God's word and wisdom, the instrument of creation, and even a second God and a 'son' of God. Justin took up these connections and ascribed *personality* to the Logos. For Justin the universal principle by which all men know the truth and the good is the divine Logos, or reason. The Logos was made, or begotten, by God before everything else, was necessary to mediate in subsequent creation. The Logos, the pre-existent Christ, came down from heaven as a spirit and made himself one with the flesh conceived of Mary (Justin did not distinguish sharply

23 Bernard, *Oneness and Trinity*, p65.

between the Word and the Spirit). He described the Logos as 'another God', but qualified it by saying 'in number, but not in will'.

The resulting doctrine is therefore *binitarian*; there are two divine beings, the supreme God ('the Father') and the Logos ('the Son'). It is also *subordinationist*, as the Logos is seen to have a secondary or inferior status. Sometimes there was no clear distinction made by the Apologists between the Logos and the Spirit[xviii]. For Justin, the New Testament use of 'The Father' refers to God transcendent, God removed from the world (like Plato's supreme God). 'The Son' refers to God immanent, God in the world, and is identical with the Logos. Justin described the Logos as 'Light of Light', or 'as one torch lit from another'.

The Logos concept dominated the theology of the Godhead from the time of Justin onwards, at least in the Greek-speaking east, until the establishment of the Trinity doctrine in the fourth century. It fitted naturally into a pagan cast of mind. Converts from paganism could relate naturally to the Logos as a separate being from the 'supreme God'. More generally, converts coming from belief in many gods would see nothing wrong in Christianity having two divine persons. This was shown by the popularity in the fourth century of Arianism, a theology similar to that of Justin in the sense of having two objects of worship.

Mackintosh, in *The Person of Jesus Christ*, criticises the Logos doctrine for its replacement of the New Testament revelation of Christ as the Son of God with a concept of Logos independent of scripture, and of the subordination of the Son to the Father with a philosophical dualism:

> The introduction of the Logos-conception was a dubious expedient, and before long it was to prove itself a weapon which men grasped only by the blade … In St John the term Logos is obviously defined by relation to the more fundamental 'Son' ... in the Apologists this relation is turned the other way. Here 'Logos' comes onto the scene with a settled independent meaning of its own ... Christ is before all things the Logos, rather than the Son of God ... Further, if the Logos be defined as **caused** by God, it becomes plain that (authentic New Testament) subordination is on the point of passing into essential dualism and inferiority[24]

Geoffrey Lampe, sometime Regius Professor of Divinity at Cambridge University, identified what he called a 'double projection' whereby the personality of Jesus Christ was (wrongly) transferred by theologians of the Early

---

[24] H.R. Mackintosh, *The Doctrine of the Person of Jesus Christ*, pp142f.

Church to a pre-existent 'Eternal Son'. Lampe argues that this concept denies the true humanity of Jesus:

> The Christological concept of the pre-existent divine Son ... reduces the real, socially and culturally conditioned, personality of Jesus to the metaphysical abstraction, 'human nature'... According to this Christology, the eternal Son assumes a timeless human nature (which) corresponds to nothing in the actual concrete world; Jesus Christ has not, after all, really 'come in the flesh'[25]

In the first 'projection', the personality of Jesus was projected onto the Logos, and the Logos was then called 'the Son'. As Lampe puts it:

> The adoption of the concept of the pre-existent Son as the dominant model for Christology meant ... that the Logos became conceptualised in human terms as Jesus.[26]

The second 'projection' was to project the personality of this supposed Eternal Son back into the earthly life of Jesus, and to interpret sayings of Jesus such as "I came down from heaven ..." (John 6:38) in terms of a life that the Eternal Son was supposed to have lived before the Incarnation.

The Logos doctrine was hugely influential in the later development of the doctrine of the Trinity. Justin himself seems to have been a binitarian[xix], but Theophilus and Athenagoras used the Greek word 'triad', or trinity, for God. Theophilus wrote in one instance of the first three days of creation being types for the 'triados' of God, and his Word, and his Wisdom. Athenagoras wrote of God as 'triad', made up of Father, Logos and Spirit; both Logos and Spirit emanating (issuing) from the Father. It is inconceivable that the Trinity doctrine could have developed without the Logos theology.

Principles of the Apologists

- **One supreme God**
- **The *Logos* a 'second' divine figure**
- **Philosophy and cosmology more important than scripture**

---

25 G. Lampe, *God as Spirit*, p144.

26 G. Lampe, *God as Spirit*, p135.

Logos doctrine (AD130-180)

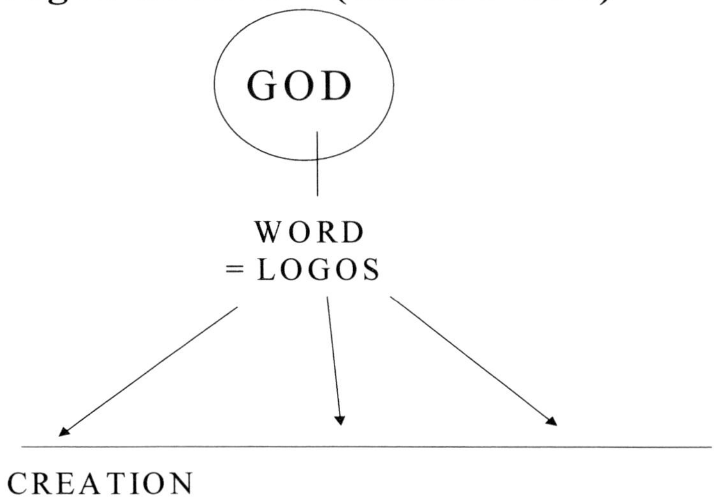

Irenaeus (AD 180-200)

Irenaeus Bishop of Lyon was the first major church theologian of the post-apostolic period. He put great effort into the refutation of gnosticism. His major work was *Against Heresies* (c185). He contrasted the unchanging and unified church with leadership descended from the apostles with the fragmented gnostic schools. In the controversies over the determination of the canon of scripture, he was the first to give criteria[xx] by which texts can be accepted as authoritative. He emphasized the continuity between the Old and the New Testaments, as evidenced by the fulfilment of prophecy in Jesus. He saw salvation as man's recovery of the original image of God, as in Adam before the Fall.

In his theology of the Godhead, Irenaeus was heavily influenced by Justin. He inherited the subordinationism of two divine beings, the supreme God (the Father) and divine Logos (the Son), agent of creation. However he rejected the other principle of the Apologists and based his arguments on scripture, not philosophy. He rejected the unbiblical notion that the Logos was itself created. The Logos is *eternal*, always with the Father. He used the biblical term 'the Son' in preference to 'the Logos', but uses the two as having the same meaning. Therefore he, like later trinitarians, would see the Incarnation in terms of the eternal Son descending to earth and taking a body.

> The Word of God ... became incarnate when the fulness of time had come, at which the Son of God had to become the Son of man[27]

Despite the apparent dualism, Irenaeus also insisted that God was one, and that the Son was fully God. He taught that worship was due to both God and the Son.

> The Word of God is eternal ... and is God himself[28]

> The Father is the invisible of the Son, but the Son the visible of the Father[29]

Irenaeus believed also in the complete humanity of Christ, and taught that our salvation comes from being made partakers of the divine nature through our union with Him, the second Adam.

Although Irenaeus could be said to be the first major binitarian theologian of the church, he also spoke of one God in *threefold* revelation. He expressed his faith in a threefold way, in an early trinitarian statement of belief[30]:

> This is the rule of our faith ... *God the Father* uncreated, who is uncontained, invisible, one God, creator of the universe; this is the first article of our faith ... and *the Word of God*, the Son of God, our Lord Jesus Christ ... who, in the fulness of time, in order to gather all things to himself, he became a human being amongst human beings ... to destroy death, bring life, and restore fellowship between God and humanity. And ... *the Holy Spirit* ... who, in the fulness of time was poured out in a new way on our human nature in order to renew humanity ...

Irenaeus originated the phrase 'God's economy (Greek *oikonomia*) of salvation', from which the term the 'economic Trinity' is derived. This is the term given to the view of the Trinity whereby the three Persons are seen as fulfilling different roles in salvation and revelation, according to scripture. In an 'economic'

---

27 Irenaeus, *Against Heresies* 3:16:7.

28 Irenaeus, *Against Heresies* 2:13:8.

29 Irenaeus, *Against Heresies* 4:6:6.

30 Irenaeus, *Demonstration of the Apostolic Preaching*, quoted in McGrath, op cit, p296.

Trinity, the Father comes first as the author of all, and the Son and the Spirit come second and third, accomplishing mediating or revelationary roles.

Irenaeus also seems to have held some beliefs compatible with those later 'modalists' or 'Sabellians' who opposed a Trinity. For instance there is evidence[31] to suggest that if Irenaeus taught a distinction of persons within the Godhead, then it was a *temporary* distinction, to be extinguished when the Son delivers up the kingdom to the Father (1 Corinthians 15:24-28). This was the position of Marcellus Bishop of Ancyra, who was exiled in the 4th century for his adherence to the creed of Nicea and supposed modalism.

<u>The binitarian theology of Irenaeus</u>

Binitarianism(AD180-200)

Irenaeus

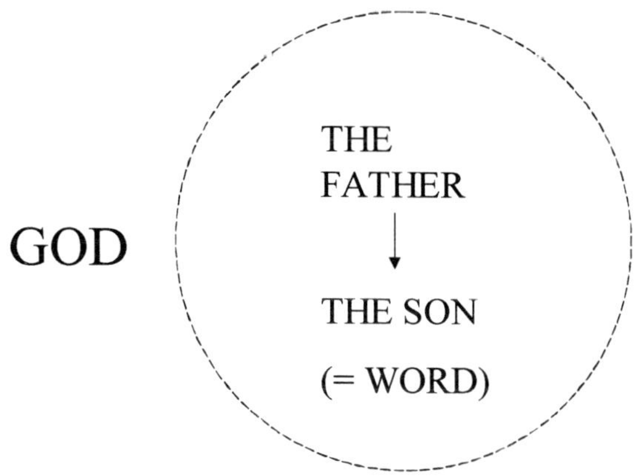

[31] Irenaeus, *Against Heresies* 5:36:1-2. Bernard (p100) quotes Heick on Irenaeus' teaching 'After the mission of Christ is accomplished, Christ's special position in the economy of the Trinity will cease ... there is a Trinity for the purpose of revelation only. After all has been accomplished, the distinction between the persons will cease'.

The first trinitarians (AD 200-250)

It has already been noted that the doctrine of the Trinity is not to be found explicitly in the New Testament. Nor is there any explicit evidence that Jesus regarded himself as part of a Trinity, although trinitarians of course maintain that the doctrine is to be found *implicitly* in the Bible (see Chapter 3). The Trinity doctrine was developed in succession to the binitarian theology of Irenaeus and the Apologists during the course of the 3rd and 4th centuries. This development owed something to pagan philosophical concepts and traditions; for example Justin and the trinitarians Clement and Origen (in different ways) were heavily influenced by Platonism, and Tertullian was a Stoic before he became a Christian.

The first recorded theologian to formulate the doctrine of the Trinity was Tertullian, a rhetorician and lawyer originally from Carthage but based in Rome. He was well educated in Greek philosophy, and his debt to Stoicism shows in his writings. He wrote in Latin (the first major theologian to do so). Converted around 195, he was at first apparently a binitarian, inheriting the Logos doctrine from the Apologists. In about 207 Tertullian converted to Montanism, a sect that emphasized spiritual gifts, and to whom the Holy Spirit, the Paraclete, was a substantial divine Person in its own right (he later left the Church over its refusal to recognise Montanism). It is understandable therefore that Tertullian would have believed in three distinct divine persons. However Tertullian was also a firm believer in the unity of God. The consequence was the first attempt to define God in terms of three persons, but only one being or substance. In Latin the formula was *una substantia, tres personae.* However this formula obscures the subordinationism that Tertullian inherited from the Apologists. The three 'persons' are not equal at all. Indeed he tends to use 'person' only for the second and third in the Trinity (Logos and Spirit), as a description of the personal way in which the divine 'substance' is manifested (the Latin word *persona* is close in meaning to a mask or appearance). His use of 'substance' is materialist, reflecting the Stoic influence.

Tertullian tried to reconcile the subordinationism of the Logos theology with the unity of God and the deity of Christ. He was energetic in his attacks on the modalists (see below) who denied the distinction between Father and Son in the interests of the unity of God. Whilst agreeing with them that God was one and that Christ was God, he defended vigorously the distinction between the Father and the Son. The Father was the whole substance of God, but the Son was a *subordinate* portion (apparently contradicting Colossians 2:9). The Son could only be called 'God' in the absence of the Father, just as a sunbeam could be called 'sun' but not in comparison to the sun itself. The Spirit was in third place.

The Son and the Spirit have the second and third places assigned to them[32]

Tertullian followed Irenaeus in seeing the 'threeness' of God as a 'divine economy', the working out of God's plan in history. He believed that the Trinity was temporary, with a beginning and an ending. The beginning of the Son he identified with 'Let there be light' (Genesis 1:3) when the Father sends out His Word for the first time, and with Proverbs 8:22f. Before that time God was on his own, and could not be called 'the Father' until there was a Son. After being begotten the Son aided the Father in creation[xxi].

Although Tertullian believed that Christ was fully man, he insisted that Christ had two distinct natures or substances, spirit (or the Word), and flesh (or humanity), each acting independently[xxii]. If the two natures joined together, they would both lose their distinctive character. Tertullian was the first theologian to use Matthew 28:19 as a baptism formula, and taught immersion three times, once for each person of the Trinity. His doctrine was disseminated in the west through the *De Trinitate*, written around 250 by the Roman presbyter Novatian[xxiii].

Hippolytus was a contemporary of Tertullian and wrote in similar terms of the Trinity, although in Greek (the last western theologian to do so).

A contemporary of Tertullian in the east was Clement of Alexandria (active from 190 to about AD 216). Clement was a pagan philosopher before his conversion, and always retained an admiration for Greek philosophy. He became a teacher at the Catechetical School in Alexandria, having been a pupil there. He was heavily influenced by the Apologists Tatian and Justin, and his theology was, naturally, dominated by the Logos doctrine. With Clement, like the Apologists, the eternal Logos takes priority over the human Jesus, although, also like the Apologists, he calls the Logos 'the Son'. He held that the Logos was different when viewed from above by the Father from when viewed from below by man. From above, he is the highest below the Father. From below he appears as the fulness of the Godhead. Clement attempted to claim both the full equality of Father and Son, and also the subordination of the Son[33]

---

32 Tertullian, *Against Praxeas 3.*

33 Mackintosh (p163) suggests that for Clement the equality of Father and Son comes first, and the idea of subordination is secondary.

Origen (died 254) was Clement's pupil and his successor in the Catechetical School, but much less sympathetic to pagan philosophy and ideas (although probably still unconciously influenced by Plato)[34]. He developed the Logos theology to its furthest logical extent. He brought in the idea of *the eternal Son.* According to him, the eternal Son was 'a second God', subordinate to the Father and not as good. He has the same nature (Greek *homoousios*, 'homo' meaning same, 'ousios' meaning nature or essence) but a different substance (Greek *hypostasis*). The Son was not born at a single moment, but is eternally being generated. The human soul of Jesus was fused with the Logos prior to His birth. Origen's followers used a trinitarian baptismal formula. The further development of trinitarianism owes much to Origen, although he was later condemned a heretic for his belief in the pre-existence of souls and in the possible salvation of the devil.

The subordinate Trinity of the first trinitarians

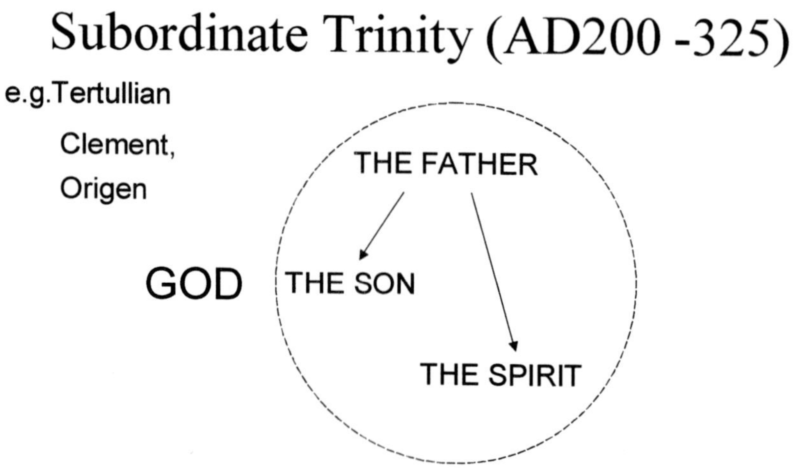

[34] Henry Chadwick, *The Early Church*, p101.

Modalism versus trinitarianism (AD 200-250)

In the first part of the third century AD a controversy arose between between the emerging trinitarian theology and non-trinitarian views. The debate was known as the monarchian controversy. Monarchianism is the name given to views that try to safeguard the unity (or the monarchy) of God.

To the monarchians the Logos theology posed a clear threat to the unity of God. There were two types of monarchian view. *Dynamic monarchianism* or *adoptionism* was the view that Jesus was only a man, who was filled with divine power at baptism. *Modalistic monarchianism*, also termed *modalism*, is the view that the one, undivided, God appears in different ways (or modes). Jesus Christ was one of the modes, or appearances, of the one God. The early trinitarians attacked monarchianism in defence of the Logos Christology and of the distinction between Father and Son.

Discussion of these doctrinal debates in the early church is complicated by three factors. Firstly theologians often held views that cannot easily be pigeon-holed into neat categories.

Secondly, the Greek and Latin words for the key words like 'essence', 'nature', 'substance', 'person' are subject to differences of interpretation. Greek was the language of the Eastern Roman Empire, but Latin was the dominant language in the West after AD 250[xxiv]. The difference in language was a source of misunderstandings between East and West. The Arian controversy in the fourth century was very much an Eastern affair, and Westerners often apparently had difficulty seeing what the problem was. (See next section for a discussion of the terms).

Thirdly there are no surviving documents from non-trinitarians or modalists. All that we know of them are quotes used and references made by their opponents.

It seems that popular sympathy was with modalism. The trinitarian theologian Origen writes on classes of believer, of whom the first class have faith in both God and the Word, and the second:

> ... who know nothing but Jesus Christ and him crucified, considering that the Word made flesh is the whole Word, and knowing only Christ after the flesh. Such is the great multitude of those who are counted believers.[35]

Modalistic monarchianism came to prominence in the late second century AD. The movement was apparently based in Rome, and had popular support for at least a generation. Three successive bishops, Victor (189-199), Zephyrinus (199-217) and Callistus (217-223), were supporters, at least to some extent. Principal spokesmen were Noetus of Smyrna, Praxeas of Asia Minor and Sabellius of Libya. They held that Father, Son and Holy Spirit are descriptions of God in different relationships or roles, not different divine persons. The analogy is made with a man who is variously father, son and friend to different people, but is nevertheless the same person all the time. None of their writings survive, and what is known survives in the form of quotes from their trinitarian opponents, Tertullian of Carthage and Hippolytus of Rome.

Our information about Praxeas comes from Tertullian in his *Against Praxeas*. According to him Praxeas came from Asia Minor to Rome in about 190. He indicates that the modalistic doctrine had spread everywhere, and that a majority of believers preferred it to trinitarianism, because it appeared to support monotheism. Apparently Praxeas accused trinitarians of teaching two or three gods. According to Tertullian:

> (Praxeas and his followers think) that one cannot believe in one only God in any other way than by saying that the Father, the Son and the Holy Ghost are the very selfsame Person ...
>
> He (Praxeas) says that the Father Himself came down into the Virgin, was himself born of her, Himself suffered, indeed was Himself Jesus Christ" [36]

If Jesus Christ is the Father, then of course it was the Father who suffered on the Cross. Critics called this view *patripassionism*, accusing it of saying that the Father died on the Cross.

Praxeas apparently opposed the sect of Montanism, which emphasized prophecy and the gifts of the Spirit, and to which Tertullian belonged. Hence Tertullian's well-known statement about Praxeas:

---

[35] Origen, *Commentary on John* 2:3, quoted in Bernard p139.

[36] Tertullian, *Against Praxeas* 2 and *Against Praxeas* 1, quoted in Bernard pp146f.

> Praxeas managed two businesses for the devil in Rome. He drove out prophecy and brought in heresy, put to flight the Paraclete and crucified the Father.

Most information we have about Noetus comes from the trinitarian Hippolytus. Noetus apparently came from Smyrna in Asia Minor, and he founded a theological school in Rome around 200. Hippolytus notes the prevalence of Modalism in Rome and blames the two bishops Zephyrinus and Callistus for encouraging it. As with Praxeas, Noetus held that that Father and the Son are the same entity. According to Hippolytus:

> Noetus affirms that the Son and the Father are the same ... he thinks to establish the sovereignty of God, alleging that Father and Son, so called, are one and the same (substance), not one individual produced from a different one, but Himself from Himself; and that He is styled by name Father and Son, according to the vicissitude of times[37]

Hippolytus repeats the accusation of patripassionism made by Tertullian against Praxeas:

> (Noetus) alleged that Christ was the Father Himself, and that the Father Himself was born, and suffered, and died[38]

Sabellius of Libya is particularly associated with the specific belief that God was revealed as Father in creation, as Son in redemption and as the Holy Spirit in regeneration. It is possible that he believed that the different roles were confined to different time frames: God was Father in the Old Testament period, Son in the New Testament period, and Spirit in the church age. Modalistic monarchianism subsequently became described as Sabellianism.

The bishops Zephyrinus and Callistus also came in for comment and attack from Hippolytus for their modalism. Bernard points out[39] that the Roman Catholic Church considers Zephyrinus to be a pope, and holds that an official doctrinal pronouncement by a pope is infallible. Yet at least two bishops of Rome endorsed modalism, and these bishops no doubt considered that to be consistent with their predecessors as bishops of Rome.

---

37 Hippolytus, *Refutation of all Heresies* 9:5, quoted in Bernard p150.

38 Hippolytus, *Against the Heresy of one Noetus* 1, quoted in Bernard p151.

39 D. Bernard, *Oneness and Trinity*, p153.

A crucial issue for Sabellianism is the identity of the Son. If, as modalists say, 'the Father' is just another term for God, and the Spirit refers to God's nature as spirit, who is the Son and how is the distinction between Father and Son to be explained? To say 'Jesus is God' without any qualification does not account for the real personal distinction between Jesus and the Father shown in the New Testament. How can Jesus be God if he prayed to God? Did he pray to himself? How can Jesus be the Father when he said "the Father is greater than I" (John 14:28).

Praxeas apparently interpreted the distinction between Father and Son along the lines of the Father being the invisible Spirit (John 4:24), and *the Son being the manifestation in flesh*, but both constituting one person. The Holy Spirit is not a third person, but just refers to God's nature as spirit. Thus, Tertullulian commented on Praxeas and his followers:

> All in one person, they distinguish two, Father and Son, understanding the Son to be flesh, that is man, that is Jesus; and the Father to be spirit, that is God, ... therefore ... it must be the flesh that is the Son of God[40]

According to Hippolytus Callistus acknowledged a real distinction between Father and Son. The difference was that 'the Father' was the name for the divine Spirit indwelling 'the Son', who is the human body, the flesh, of Jesus. Hippolytus commented:

> Callistus ... maintains that the Father is not one person and the Son another, but that they are one and the same ... and he affirms that the Spirit, which became incarnate in the virgin, is not different from the Father, but one and the same ... for that which is seen, which is man, he considers to be the Son; whereas the Spirit, which was contained in the Son, to be the Father[41]

Bernard concludes that the consensual 'answer' from the modalists appears to have been that 'the Son' refers to the humanity of Christ, with the deity of Christ identified as 'the Father', or as the indwelling Spirit.

Although modalistic monarchianism was clearly popular, at least in the West, it seems to have declined in importance during the third century. By the time of the Council of Nicaea in 325, the Logos doctrine and the emerging trinitarian

---

40 Tertullian, *Against Praxeas* 27, quoted in Bernard p147.

41 Hippolytus, *Refutation of all Heresies* 9:8, quoted in Bernard p151. Hippolytus accused Callistus of trying to compromise between modalism and distinctions proper to a Logos theology, but Bernard concludes that the views attributed to Callistus on this question are probably representative of the other modalists.

theology appear to have been dominant amongst theologians. However the Council of Nicaea was very much an Eastern affair, and modalistic monarchianism may have still been a current viewpoint in the west. Nevertheless no more is heard of modalistic monarchianism after the third century.

Why did modalistic monarchianism decline? Particularly in the East, there was a fear of defining a doctrine which could be interpreted as dispensing with the distinction between the Father and the Son. The Son prays to the Father, is subordinate to the Father, knows less than the Father and so on. The problem of accounting for the Father/Son distinction is perhaps the greatest problem facing any modalist or non-trinitarian theology[42]. A closely related issue is the status of the ascended Christ. It seems that modalists said that on his ascension the Son is 'absorbed' back into the Father, which appears to conflict with biblical evidence of the Ascended Christ being separate from the Father in heaven (e.g. Acts 7:56). We do not know what Sabellius and his colleagues had to say on this point.

Although modalism as such may have as such disappeared from official view after the third century, the arguments and issues surrounding the Logos Christology and the Godhead did not go away. In the decade following the Council of Nicaea Bishops Eustace of Antioch and Marcellus of Ancyra, were exiled for their hostility to the trinitarian theology of Origen and their suspected Sabellianism. At Antioch in 362 there were three rivals for the bishopric; of these Paulinus, a follower of Marcellus, was recognised by Rome and Alexandria as the true bishop[xxv].

Into the fourth century and beyond, modalism continued to excite suspicion and fear. The creeds agreed at the Council of Nicaea in 325 and of Constantinople in 381 were explicitly formulated to exclude Sabellianism.

The Arian controversy

The Emperor Constantine on his accession at the beginning of the fourth century had converted to Christianity and made it the state religion. From that time onwards the Roman emperors would exercise great influence over the Church and over the development of Christian doctrine. Christianity was now the 'official' religion of the Empire.

---

[42] Although the trinitarian view also has difficulties. See Chapter 5.

The Arian controversy divided the Christian establishment for most of the fourth century and the issues raised are still relevant to this day.

The dispute started in about AD 318 in Alexandria with an argument between Arius, a presbyter and his bishop Alexander. From the beginning it was an Eastern affair[xxvi]. Arius highlighted the contradictions and difficulties of the emerging 'subordinationist' trinitarianism of Tertullian and Origen. How could Jesus be God, yet different from 'God? How could Jesus be both God and man? How can God be one and also three? He attempted to resolve these contradictions by saying:

1. *God is absolutely one and immutable (incapable of change).*

2. *Christ is the first of all created beings, the agent of creation on behalf of the One Supreme God, unlike in essence from God.*

The Arian 'solution' was logically appealling. The Arian conception of Christ appears to fit with the biblical portrait of Jesus who showed human weakness, exercised divine powers at times, but was always subordinate to God. It could be argued that Arianism is no more than taking the subordinationism of Tertullian and Origen to its logical conclusion.

It is difficult to distinguish what Arius actually believed from what his later followers claimed. None of his writings survive, and all that is known of them is from quotations used by his opponents. The modern view of the Arian Christ is of a secondary deity, divine but of lower rank than the Supreme God, neither man nor God but somewhere in between. Arius' followers claimed full divinity for Christ, despite his not have the same nature as God. Some would interpret Arius as saying that Jesus was fully human while on earth[43].

Most theologians nowadays would argue that Arianism was fatally flawed because it had a 'saviour' who could not save. The argument is that Christ has to be both fully God and fully man, not 'something in between'. If the Arian Christ were not fully human, his death could have no significance for humans. If he were no more than a created being (so it is said) he could not be the Word made flesh (John 1:14) or 'so much better than the angels' (Hebrews 1:4). Mackintosh summarises these criticisms:

---

[43] Associated Bible Students in *The Doctrine of Christ* disagree with the criticisms, arguing that Jesus' pre-existence as a spirit being does not preclude his full humanity while on earth. They also question why a created being could not be 'so much better than the angels'.

> The completeness with which Arius missed his mark is one of the ironies of history. Starting from a desire to clear the worship of Christ from a charge of polytheism, he led the way back to heathen idolatry. After proclaiming that Christ's humanity is fundamental, he ended by denying him a human soul. Above all, he made it fatally certain that on his terms our Lord is no true mediator who can lay a hand on us both. [44]

On this view, Arianism maintained the unity of God and the distinction between the Father and the Son at the expense of both the humanity and the deity of Christ. Because it was clearly binitarian, Arianism appealed to converts who had recently come out of paganism. The Goths encamped around the northern border of the Empire converted easily to Arianism.

The Arian doctrine also gained initial popularity amongst bishops and presbyters, such as Eusebius Bishop of Nicomedia, because it seemed to maintain the unity of God without being Sabellian. Because Arianism can be seen as taking the doctrine of a subordinationist Trinity to its logical conclusion, it was thought by its opponents that it could only be defeated by formulas that emphasize the unity of Father and Son, while recognising the distinction between them. After over 60 years of controversy Arianism was defeated in Church Councils by the formulas of the classical Trinity.

The Council of Nicaea and Athanasius

The Emperor Constantine was determined to end the dispute over Arianism, and called a council of bishops in Nicaea in Bythnia in AD 325. This was the first ecumenical council of the church. About 220 bishops attended, all but a handful from the East. Athanasius, the man who was to succeed Alexander as Bishop of Alexandria and who was to play a central role in the Arian controversy, attended as secretary to Alexander and according to reports played a leading role in the debates.

At the Council, a creed was formulated which explicitly refuted Arianism. Of Christ, it included the phrases 'begotten not made', 'of one substance (*homoousion*) with the Father' and 'was made flesh, was made man' (these remain in the so-called Nicene creed used today). The Emperor indicated his approval, and it was forced through, with only a few refusing to sign. However there

[44] Mackintosh, *op cit*, p178.

were many secret dissenters, and it was not until the Council of Constantinople in 381 that the issue was finally settled. Athanasius himself was banished five times at times when the Arian party became dominant, finally being reinstated about 362.

Athanasius maintained the unity of God and also the full divinity and humanity of Christ. For him, the Son has the same nature as the Father, and is not an arbitrary creature (or even offspring). He reconciled the *homoousion* of Father and Son with the distinction between them by using the familiar image of *generation* (used by Tertullian and Origen). The Son is generated from the Father and is related to the Father as a ray of light is to the source. Athanasius argued that if the Son has a created nature, his becoming man leaves us still at a distance from God, for no one who is a creature like ourselves could raise us to oneness with the Creator. He argued that if God needed a mediator to create, and the Logos is a creature, then another mediator would have been required to create the Logos, and so on.

Christ's humanity was as necessary for Athanasius as his divinity. He wrote 'He was made man, that we might be made God'. He dispensed with the idea of the mediating Logos and returned to the biblical Christ, who suffered, died and was raised from the dead. Through Christ, the second Adam, humanity is able to participate in the divine nature. It is perhaps incorrect to see Athanasius as the protagonist of the Trinity doctrine, as he is commonly described, but more accurate to describe him as the defender of monotheism and the doctrine of a Saviour who is both God and man.

It is customary to see the Council of Nicaea as the foundation of trinitarianism in the church. However its purpose was not to debate the Trinity but the status of the Son. Indeed, the status of the Holy Spirit was barely mentioned in the final statement. The creed was attacked by its critics as Sabellian, because of the emphasis on the identity of nature between the Father and the Son.

One of those attacked along with Athanasius was Marcellus Bishop of Ancyra, one of the participants of the Council of Nicaea and a supporter of the agreed creed. Marcellus put forward views that are close to modalism without being consciously Sabellian. He emphasized the unity of God, and that the Logos and Spirit came forth from God at particular times in accordance with his plan. He held that the Son came into being with the birth of Jesus, and that the Spirit exists only since Christ breathed it on the disciples (John 20:21). Marcellus is quoted[45]:

> The Word as such is pure spirit, and only became the Son of God by becoming the Son of Man

Marcellus quoted 1 Corinthians15:24ff to show that any distinction between Son and Father is only temporary and relative to the created order. After the Second Coming the Sonship will end, and the Logos will merge back into God. Athanasius and Marcellus were exiled to the West together in AD 336, and they were welcomed to communion in Rome by Bishop Julius.

It is perhaps worthy of notice that in the creed agreed at Nicaea there is no mention of the Logos. The Logos theology, along with Origen's eternal generation of the Son, by now had largely disappeared from official doctrine. However it had left behind the legacy of the notion of the 'Eternal Son', and what would soon become the official trinitarian doctrine of three co-essential and co-equal beings.

The new trinitarianism: the 'three in one' formula

For nearly 60 years after the Nicene Council there was a dispute between three parties:

1) The 'right wing' or 'same nature' party (including Athanasius) holding to the official Nicene statement holding that the Son has the same nature (*homoousios*) as the Father.

2) The 'middle ground' or 'like nature' party (homoiousians) founded in 358, led by Basil Bishop of Ancyra, holding that 'the Son is like the Father in all things, as the Holy Scriptures say and teach'.

3) The 'left wing', 'unlike nature', Arianising party (anhomoeans), led by Eunomius among others, holding that the Son, as a created (though divine) being, cannot be like the Father at all.

Compromises were made between the first two parties that eventually resulted at a new formulation of the Trinity doctrine. The controversy was effectively settled against Arianism at the Council of Alexandria in 362 when Athanasius

---

[45] Mackintosh, *op cit*, p190.

(reinstated from exile) of the Nicene party reached agreement with the homoiousians, led by Basil of Ancyra. Athanasius recognised that the latter meant by 'like nature' something quite close to the 'same nature' of the Nicene definition.

There were issues about the status of the Spirit. If the Father and the Son had the same nature, did the Spirit share that nature or was it some sort of angelic being? If the Son was a lesser being than the Father, did the Spirit come lower still? In order to defend the *homoousios* definition and the creed of Nicaea against Arianism, both Basil and Athanasius felt obliged to include the Spirit as having the same nature as the Son and the Father.

The distinction was now made between the use of *ousia*, meaning nature (Latin *substantia*), and *hypostasis*, meaning person (Latin *persona*) (previously the terms had been used without that clear distinction). The formula:

One nature, three persons

was used to describe the Godhead. The trinitarian formula was now available in Greek for the Eastern Roman Empire and in Latin for the Western, but the terms did not carry exactly the same meanings in each language. The term *persona* suggests something more insubstantial than *hypostasis*. The latter means something that stands by itself, can support itself, whereas *persona* means something more like a mask or a role. In future interpretations of the same formula, the West tended to emphasize more the unity of God, and see the differences between the persons of the Trinity more along the lines of modalism. On the other hand the East tended to emphasize more the separateness of the persons.

The theologians who continued the work of Basil of Ancyra and Athanasius are known as the younger Nicene party, headed by the Cappadocian Fathers: Basil of Caesarea (died 379), his brother Gregory of Nyssa (died after 394), and Gregory of Nazianzus (died 389). They can perhaps be considered the founders of trinitarianism, in the sense that their formulations of the doctrine were the first to become accepted by an ecumenical council (that of Constantinople in 381). They interpreted the theology of Athanasius in the direction of three co-equal Persons sharing the same essence, but who are distinct, yet not separable.

For the new trinitarian logic, divine works prove divine status, and divine status implies *equal* divine status. So if the Spirit is responsible for divine works, it (or he) must be a third Person in the Godhead[xxvii].

This quote from Gregory of Nazianzus shows how the Cappadocian Fathers understood the development of the doctrine of the Trinity as a gradual revelation. First the Old Testament had to be accepted as showing the Father as God. Then the Son had to be admitted as fully divine. Only then could the full divinity of the Holy Spirit be admitted:

> The Old Testament preached the Father openly and the Son more obscurely. The New Testament revealed the Son, and hinted at the divinity of the Holy Spirit. Now the Spirit dwells in us, and is revealed more clearly to us. It was not proper to preach the Son openly, while the divinity of the Father had not yet been admitted. Nor was it proper to accept the Holy Spirit before [the divinity of] the Son had been acknowledged … Instead, by gradual advances and … partial ascents, we should move forward and increase in clarity, so that the light of the Trinity should shine[46]

Mackintosh describes how the Cappadocians reinterpreted the 'three-in-one' formula:

> 'Ousia' now received a significance midway between the abstract 'essence' and the concrete 'individual', yet so that it inclined very strongly to the former; 'hypostasis' was placed in meaning midway between 'person' and 'quality' ('accident' or 'mode'), yet so that the personal idea was the stronger[47]

Therefore the emphasis became much more on the 'threeness' in the Trinity than on the 'oneness'. Mackintosh continues:

> Starting as they did from the threeness in the divine, with the unity as a mysterious problem, it was particularly difficult to avoid the semblance of tritheism, and this was an accusation long current in the West [48]

This 'new' doctrine of the Trinity had important differences from the older formulations[xxviii]. The binitarianism of the Apologists and the trinitarianism of Tertullian and Origen were subordinationist. For them the Logos and the Spirit were generated from the Father (or supreme God) and were subordinate to the Father. Although this subordinationism seemed to threaten the unity of God, it had some biblical basis because it reflected the subordination of Jesus and the Spirit to God shown in the New Testament. Because the new trinitarians were forced under the attack of Arianism to emphasize the sameness of nature and

---

46 Gregory of Nazianzus, *Theological Oration*, McGrath, *The Christian Theology Reader*, pp184-5.

47 Harnack, *Grundriss*, p182, quoted in Mackintosh, ibid, p193.

48 Mackintosh, ibid, p194.

equality of the three Persons, the problems of subordinationism were replaced by a new problem:

How to account for the distinctions and relations between the co-equal Persons of the Trinity?

Previously, the Son was described as having been 'generated' by the Father, but of the same essence, and this could be understood in terms of the human example of a son being generated from his father but having the same nature. If the Spirit was to be included as well, there arises the problem of distinguishing the Son from the Spirit if they are both equally 'generated'. If all three Persons share equally in the divine essence, and none of them generate any of the others, how are they to be distinguished? And if we are now including the Spirit as a third divine Person, how do we know that there are no more than three? Why not, say, include God's Wisdom as a fourth member of the Godhead? On this problem Mackey writes:

> ... formulae which are designed to answer the twin questions 'one what?' and 'three what?' are inevitably constructed of such general terms that they already presuppose precise answers to such questions as 'how is the one distinct from the three?' and 'how is each of the three distinct from the others?'. For only if we are already sure that we have one and *three* can we reasonably be required to trouble ourselves to say one *what* or three *what.* But ... with the growing distance from the old emanationist, subordinationist model, and its inbuilt answer to just these questions of distinction, the problem of distinction becomes more rather than less acute.[49]

The Cappadocians tried to distinguish the Persons according to their works, but this was hampered by two principles attributed to Gregory of Nyssa, intended to safeguard the unity of the Godhead and the divinity of the Persons.

The first principle is that of the 'coinherence' of the Persons (Greek *perichoresis*)[xxix], meaning that each Person is involved in whatever the others do and that they go everywhere together. The second principle, later to be known as *opera ad extra sunt indivisa* (see below), is that the works of the Persons, seen from outside, are indivisable.

These principles, while (supposedly) safeguarding the divinity of the Son and the Spirit and so the *homoousios* (sameness of essence) of the Persons, made it very difficult to distinguish their individual contributions, or indeed, to distinguish them from each other.

---

[49] J.P. Mackey, *The Christian Experience of God as Trinity*, p143.

Even though the concepts of generation and subordination were (supposedly) discarded from the Trinity, the Cappadocians still tried to use these ideas to maintain distinctions between the Persons. The Father is still regarded as the source of the Godhead. The Father *begets* the Son and *breathes* the Spirit, or the Spirit *proceeds from* the Father (John 15:26). However these images are not sufficient to define the Persons, and in particular to define the troublesome Third Person. How can the Spirit be distinguished from the Son, if both come from the Father? Gregory of Nyssa's attempt to define the Spirit ends in negative terms, as 'he simply is, without being ingenerate or only-begotten'[50]. Mackey notes that Gregory uses the relationship of God to creation to help in defining the Persons as well as 'images of origin in or from the the divinity such as Arians might have favoured'. Mackey goes on:

> And one might even begin to suspect that the older subordinationist model for distinguishing Father, Son and Spirit was making a subtle back-door entry to help with distinctions which were proving unusually difficult for the replacement model which had just ushered it out of the front door. [51]

The Cappadocians also tried to explain the new definition in terms of three different men having different personalities and the same human nature. However it is clear that this explanation also cannot bear the weight of the biblical distinctions between the Father and the Son.

Mackey comments on the general problem of the new trinitarians of distinguishing three co-equal Persons by the formula of three 'modes of being' sharing the same 'essence':

> Certainly the finding of a general formula does nothing to remove this problem, or even to alleviate it. And unless we can truly differentiate three distinct 'modes of being' from each other and from one 'something' which is not a mode of being, we shall have no warrant for issuing the formula at all.[52]

The Trinity becomes the official doctrine

In 381 the Emperor Theodosius convened a council at Constantinople. This ratified the creed[xxx] agreed at Nicaea, and condemned Sabellianism and

---

[50] J.P. Mackey, *The Christian Experience of God as Trinity*, p145.

[51] J.P. Mackey, *The Christian Experience of God as Trinity*, p146

[52] J.P. Mackey, *The Christian Experience of God as Trinity*, p143.

Arianism. The new doctrine of the Trinity, which may now be called the 'classical' Trinity, followed the lines laid down by the Cappadocian Father. The Holy Spirit was confirmed as a separate and co-equal divine person along with the Father and the Son. The Son was stated to be *begotten* from the Father, and the Holy Spirit to be *proceeding* from the Father. From that time on, the doctrine of the church was officially trinitarian.

The Classical Trinity

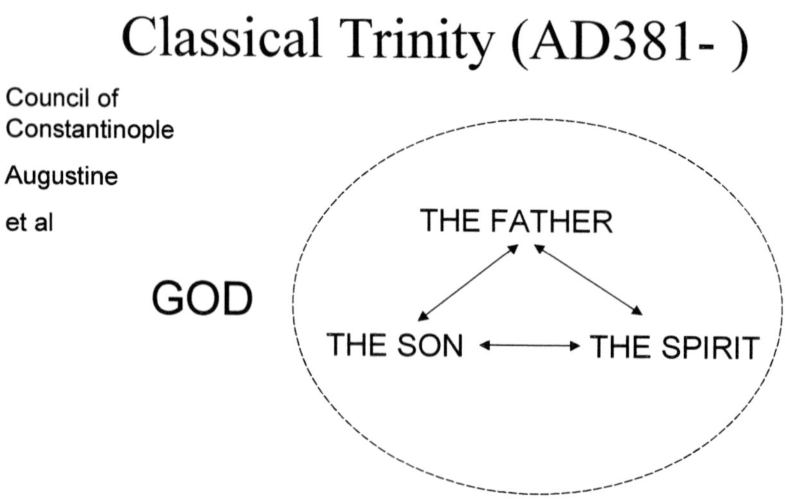

The Trinity was defined in terms of three co-equal persons, sharing the same divine nature. The concept had moved from an *'economic'* Trinity, where the Son (or Word) and Spirit were understood as being generated from God, or 'the Father', in some way, towards an *'essential'* Trinity in which the three Persons are defined in terms of their natures. However, as remarked above, the Cappadocians had already found it problematic to eliminate traces of the 'economic' Trinity from the 'essential' Trinity, and this would continue to be a problem over the coming centuries.

In the Eastern tradition the doctrine of the Trinity has remained indebted to the Constantinople definitions and the Cappadocian Fathers, with an emphasis on the distinctness of the three persons. In the West the doctrine was developed along different lines, first by Augustine and then by reformation and modern theologians. Before we consider Augustine, we note the debate over the Person of Christ that took place after Constantinople.

Debate over the Person of Christ: two natures or one?

When the debate moved from the Godhead to the Person of Christ, the belief was that Jesus was both completely human and completely divine, in other words as having *two natures*. The Council of Constantinople in 381 had accepted humanity and divinity of Jesus and confirmed the doctrine of the Trinity. The Church then entered a period of controversy over the person of Christ.

Accepting that Jesus was God, the question was asked *how* could he be divine and human at the same time? Did he have a complete divine nature and complete human nature ('100% God and 100% man')? Or does he possess some incompleteness either as a man or as God (e.g. '50% God and 50% man')? The schools of Antioch and Alexandria put forward rival viewpoints.

The emphasis of the Alexandrine school was on the divinity of Jesus and the unity of his nature. This was argued sometimes at the expense of his complete humanity or individuality, so that for instance the Alexandrian theologians might talk about the Word of God assuming human nature in general, rather than becoming an actual individual human being.

The Antiochene school emphasized the complete and individual humanity of Jesus. This carried the risk of regarding Jesus as having two completely separate natures, human and divine, with two different personalities and two different wills.

The principal protagonists of the debate were Apollinaris, Nestorius of Antioch, Cyril of Alexandria and Leo of Rome. Apollinaris of Laodicea (died c390) suggested that Jesus, like all men had a spirit, soul and body (1 Thessalonians 5:23), but that the human spirit was replaced by the Spirit of God (having earlier suggested that it was the soul that was replaced). His doctrine safeguarded the unity of Jesus' personality at the cost of his true humanity.

Nestorius, Patriarch of Constantinople in 428, following the lines of the Antiochene theology, put forward the 'two natures' doctrine. Originally concerned by the use of 'Mother of God' to describe Mary, the doctrine was an attempt to protect the humanity of Jesus from 'contamination' by his divinity and vice versa. He was concerned that the only way that Jesus could be both authentically divine and fully human was by having two independent natures. According to Nestorius the two natures were united in a loose confederation.

Bishop Cyril of Alexandria (376-444) argued fiercely against Nestorius that Jesus had to have a single divine-human nature, otherwise for instance it could be argued that only the human side of Jesus suffered and died on the Cross (which would be no redemption at all). The favourite phrases of Cyril and his followers were 'one out of two natures', and 'one incarnate nature of God the Word' (the latter inherited from Apollinaris). Cyril's doctrine appears to sacrifice the individual humanity of Jesus in order to maintain his deity. Mackintosh comments:

> For Cyril, it was not the person of a man that the Logos had assumed, but man, i.e. the qualities and attributes of human nature. This shadowy abstractness of conception was only too certain to lead men away from the historic life portrayed in the New Testament[53]

The third ecumenical council of Ephesus in 431 did not settle the dispute. It declared that the Incarnation was the union of two natures, but did not pronounce on whether Christ had one or two natures *after* the union. The arguments flared up again when one of Cyril's followers, Eutyches of Constaninople, was accused of heresy for appearing to deny the true humanity of Christ (he apparently said "My God is not of like essence with us"). Pope Leo of Rome put forward a compromise formula in 449 based upon 'two substances or natures in the one Christ'. This became the basis for the statement agreed at the fourth ecumenical council at Chalcedon in AD 451:

> Therefore ... we all confess one and same Son, our Lord Jesus Christ, the same perfect in Godhead and the same perfect in manhood, truly God and the same truly man, of a rational soul and body, co-essential (*homoousios*) with the Father according to the Godhead, and co-essential with us according to the manhood ... to be acknowledged in two natures, without confusion, without mutation, without division, without separation; the distinction of natures (*physis*) being by no means taken away by the union, but rather the property of each nature being preserved and concurring in one person (*prosopon*) and one entity (*hypostasis*).

The Chalcedon statement was a compromise. It emphasized two natures, each perfect in itself, but also emphasized a single person. It was a compromise that covered up the division between the interpretations of the followers of Cyril and those of the followers of Nestorius. It did not attempt to explain the 'mystery' of the Incarnation, but it did try to set the limits of belief about Christ by excluding 'heretical' extremes. Thus, Arianism is rejected by the statement that Christ was truly God and co-essential with the Father. Apollinarianism is rejected by Christ being 'perfect in manhood'. The interpretation of Eutyches and Cyril's followers in terms of only one nature after the union is rejected by

---

53 Mackintosh, ibid, p209.

the explicit emphasis on 'two natures without confusion'. Nestorianism is rejected by the insistence on 'one person and one entity'.

Mackintosh comments that 'this was a document approximating closely to the theology of Cyril, but the phrase 'in two natures' proves that at a critical point Western influences had triumphed'[54]. According to The *New Dictionary of Christian Theology:*

> Chalcedon broke the rules and is on the face of it a bad compromise: two natures in one person. Some modern scholars would say that this move simply indicates the logical impossibility of the project. Yet within the terms available it was the best option. Two natures were affirmed, so stressing the full humanity of Jesus at a time of pressure to lose everything in divinity. At the same time Christ is only one person - there is no duality, he is one. The oneness is described in terms of *prosopon* and *hypostasis*, another diplomatic compromise because the terms could have slightly different meanings, but the main points which faith seemed to require were made[55]

The statement of Chalcedon marked the beginning of the description of Christ as the 'God-man'. Christ was supposed to have distinct divine and human natures, but only one divine-human personality. There was no individual human personal existence. In that sense, according to Chalcedon, Christ was not a man as we are. The prices of the compromise for 'Nestorians' and 'Cyrillenes' were as follows:

1. The 'Nestorian' ('two natures') had been forced to abandon the individual human personal existence (hypostasis) of Christ.

2. The 'Cyrillene' ('one nature') had been forced to accept two natures, human and divine, after the union.

The Council of Chalcedon was not the end of the arguments. In the 5th and 6th centuries there were disputes (and street fights) in the East between Monophysites ('one nature') and Dyophysites ('two natures'). The former emphasized the agreed single divine-human *hypostasis* of Christ, but said that it meant the same as one nature, and rejected talk of two natures as Nestorianism. Some Monophysites even claimed that the human nature of Christ had no *hypostasis*, no subject or existence, of its own. Leontius of Byzantium (c485-543), an important figure in Orthodox theology, suggested that Christ's humanity does have a hypostasis but not independently of the divine Son (a position known as *enhypostatos*).

---

[54] Mackintosh, ibid, p213

[55] G. Newlands, Christology, in *A New Dictionary of Christian Theology*, pp103f.

The fifth council at Constantinople in 553 (under the influence of Emperor Justinian) reaffirmed the formula of Chalcedon but interpreted it in the direction of Cyril and Monophysitism. Christ had two natures, but they were distinguishable only in theory. Christ had no human personality. The Monophysites were not satisfied by this. To this day the Syrian Jacobites (named after a 6th century Monophysite bishop), the Armenians, Copts and Ethiopians reject Chalcedon and the two natures doctrine.

There was a further dispute in the seventh century over how many *wills* Christ had. Monothelites held to one will, and Dyothelites held to two. In 680 the sixth council at Constantinople came down on the Dyothelite side. It declared that in Christ there are two natural wills, with the human will obedient to the divine will. However despite this apparent victory for 'two natures', the East remained wedded to a 'one nature' Monophysite outlook and consequently to the impersonality of Christ. By contrast in the West, there was greater freedom to believe in Christ's 'two natures' and his real individual humanity.

Augustine of Hippo

Eastern ideas of the Trinity have remained indebted to the Cappadocian Fathers and the concept of a Trinity defined by three distinct persons. With Augustine (354-430), the movement, which had commenced with the work of the Nicene theologians, continued away from the 'economic' Trinity where the Word and Spirit are subordinate and generated from the Father, towards the 'essential' Trinity, where the persons are defined in terms of their natures. For Augustine and those who followed him, the distinctions between the persons are between *equals*, and are derived from their relations to each other. The Word and the Spirit may *appear* subordinate to the Father, but in the eternal reality the three are co-equal.

The Cappadocians had defined the Son as begotten by the Father and the Spirit as proceeding from the Father. Although they had denied that the Son and the Spirit were subordinate figures, their definitions seemed uncomfortably close to Arianism. Henry Chadwick comments:

> Augustine was anxious to eliminate every possibility of Arianism and subordinationism from his doctrine of the Trinity. Therefore the unity of

> the Trinity needed to be safeguarded by the affirmation that the Spirit proceeds from the Father *and* the Son[56]

Augustine's declaration that the Spirit proceeds from both Father *and* Son led later to the notorious *filioque* clause in Western versions of the creeds, and to the split between West and East (see below). Eastern theologians, following the Cappadocians and the Greek binitarian tradition, and finding biblical support from verses such as John 15:26, held that the Father alone was the source of divinity. Augustine cited John 20:22, where the risen Jesus breathes on the disciples to give them the Holy Spirit, as evidence that the Spirit comes from the Son as well as the Father. The references in Paul's epistles[xxxi] to the Spirit as not only the Spirit of God or of the Father but also the Spirit of Christ or of the Son provide further evidence. Thus Augustine stated[57]:

> Nor can we say that the Holy Spirit does not also proceed from the Son. After all, the Spirit is said to be the Spirit of both the Father and the Son ... [John 20:22 is cited] ... The Holy Spirit proceeds not only from the Father, but also from the Son.

For Augustine then, the Son has therefore equal rank with the Father. Augustine also identified the Son as the wisdom of God. So what then about the Spirit? How can the equality of the Spirit with the others be protected? Augustine defined the Spirit, somewhat impersonally, as Gift, or Love. McGrath comments[58] that 'the Spirit appears as a sort of glue, binding Father and Son together, and binding both to believers'

Augustine was famous for his pyschological analogies. Influenced by his neoplatonic background, he regarded the human mind as the highest part of man. As man has been made in the image of God, God should therefore have left traces of his being in the mind of man. Augustine suggested that man's mind is made of memory, intelligence and will, and this 'triad' reflects the Trinity.

Thus Augustine argues that the nature of love implies three entities, and that the mind knowing and loving itself makes each man a trinity:

---

56 Henry Chadwick, *The Early Church*, p235.

57 Augustine, *On the Trinity*, quoted in McGrath, *Christian Theology*, p315. McGrath also notes that Augustine does not give the Father and the Son equal status as progenitors of the Spirit, because the Spirit 'principally' proceeds from the Father. All that the Son has, he has from the Father when he was begotten.

58 McGrath, *Christian Theology*, p305.

> Now when I ... love anything, there are three things present: I myself, what I love, and love itself. For I cannot love love unless I love a lover; for there is no love where nothing is loved. So there are three things: the lover, the loved, and love ... In the case of the three things which the mind knows and loves itself, the trinity of mind, love and knowledge remains ... in a wonderful way, the three are inseparable from one another, and yet each one is a distinct substance, and all together are one substance or essence, even though they are said to be mutually related to each another[59]

The unity of the Godhead was paramount, at least in Western eyes. Following Augustine and Gregory of Nyssa, trinitarian theology now accepted that the operations of the Trinity, as seen from outside, could not be divided between their members. This became known as the principle of *opera ad extra sunt indivisa.*

Accompanying this principle was the doctrine of *perichoresis* (Latin *circumincessio*) or 'mutual interpenetration', which came into use in the 6th century. Each Person of the Trinity has the others dwelling inside it. Following Colossians 2:9, the fullness of the Godhead has to dwell inside each Person of the Trinity. Each Person contains, not just a part of the Godhead, but all of it. The operations of the Trinity, as seen from outside, could not then be divided between the Persons, the principle of *opera ad extra sunt indivisa.*

These principles introduced new difficulties. If God is omnipresent, and all three persons mutually coinhere (go with each other), how can we distinguish appearances of the members of the Trinity from each other? How can we distinguish, say, the voice of the Son from the voice of the Spirit? The answer of Augustine and his successors was to devise the doctrine of *appropriation.* The external accompaniments of a particular divine manifestation are 'appropriated' to a Person even though the manifestation is the work of the whole Godhead. Thus all three Persons were involved in creation. Augustine pointed out that Genesis 1:1-3 speaks of God, the Word and the Spirit being present. Nevertheless it is *appropriate* to think of creation as the work of the Father, despite all three being involved.

Mackey points out 'the rather obvious artificiality of this explanation', its contribution to the growing separation in trinitarian theology between the eternal Son and the human Jesus'[60]. He further comments that Augustine's

---

[59] Augustine, *On the Trinity*, in A. McGrath, *The Christian Theology Reader*, pp189f.

[60] Mackey, in *A New Dictionary of Christian Theology*, pp586f.

Trinity 'is no longer really a christological doctrine'[61]. The Persons are removed further away from their role in salvation, God's 'economic' order and the biblical revelation of the Son and the Father.

Augustine's theology of the Trinity, following the definitions of the Council of Constantinople, was the defining influence in Western trinitarianism.

The split between Eastern and Western Christianity

The doctrine of the Trinity was agreed by the established Church of the Roman Empire at the Council of Constantinople. The Empire at the time was in the process of being divided into two halves, the Western, governed from Rome (and subsequently Ravenna), and the Eastern, governed from the new city of Constantinople. The Church also divided into two. The Western Church was ruled from the Pope in Rome and became the Roman Catholic Church, with Latin as the official language. The Eastern Church was governed by the Patriarch of Constantinople, becoming the Orthodox Church, with Greek the official language.

The two organisations divided officially in 1054. The schism came over Augustine's doctrine of the 'double procession', that the Spirit proceeds from the Father *and the Son* (see above). The *filioque* clause came to be added to the article on the Holy Spirit in western versions of the creed agreed at Constantinople. The Eleventh Council of Toledo in 675 set out the Western view:

> We believe that the Holy Spirit, the third person in the Trinity, is God, one and equal with God the Father and God the Son, of one substance and one nature; not, however, begotten or created, but proceeding from both, and that He is the Spirit of both. We also believe that the Holy Spirit is neither unbegotten nor begotten, for if we called him 'unbegotten' we would assert two Fathers, or if we called him 'begotten', we would appear to preach two Sons. Yet He is called the Spirit not of the Father alone, nor of the Son alone, but of both Father and Son. For He does not proceed from the Father to the Son, nor from the Son to sanctify creatures, but He is shown to have proceeded from both at once, because He is known as the love or the holiness of both. Hence we believe that the Holy Spirit is sent by both, as the Son is sent by the Father. But He is not less than the Father and the Son

[61] Mackey, *The Christian Experience of God as Trinity*, p162.

> … While they are called three persons in view of their relations, we believe in one nature or substance. Although we profess three persons, we do not profess three substances, but one substance and three persons. For the Father is Father not with respect to Himself but to the Son, and the Son is Son not to Himself but in relation to the Father; and likewise the Holy Spirit is not referred to Himself but is related to the Father and the Son, inasmuch as He is called the Spirit of the Father and the Son. So when we use the term 'God', this does not express a relationship to another, as of the Father to the Son or of the Son to the Father or of the Holy Spirit to the Father and the Son, but 'God' refers to Himself only[62]

The idea that the Spirit has to proceed from the Son as well as the Father was seen in the West to be necessary in order to 'protect' both the divinity of the Son and the unity of the Godhead. The Son had to have equal rank with the Father, and therefore an equal share in the sending of the Spirit. If the Son did not do this, then the Son would be a lesser 'second' god, and the unity of the Godhead would be threatened, so the thinking went.

The East for its part was happy to keep the formulations of the Cappadocian Fathers in which the Father alone was the source of the Godhead and generated, in different ways, the Son and the Spirit. The East questioned the biblical justification for the insertion of the *filioque* clause, and the division between West and East on this issue remains to this day.

---

[62] Statement of the Eleventh Council of Toledo on the Trinity, in A. McGrath, *The Christian Theology Reader*, pp200f.

The diagrams below illustrate the Western and Eastern views of the Trinity[63].

Western model of the Trinity

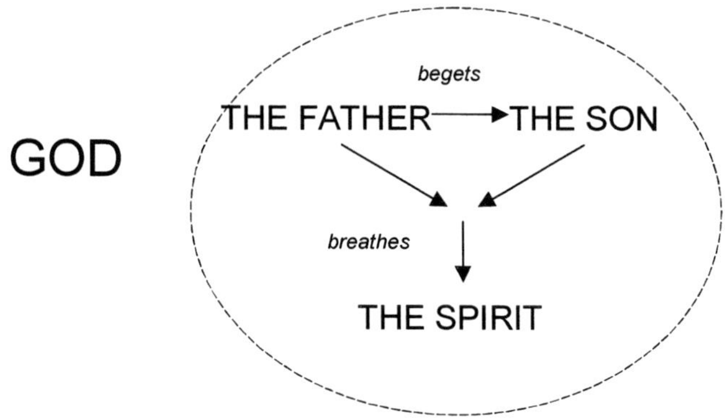

Eastern model of the Trinity

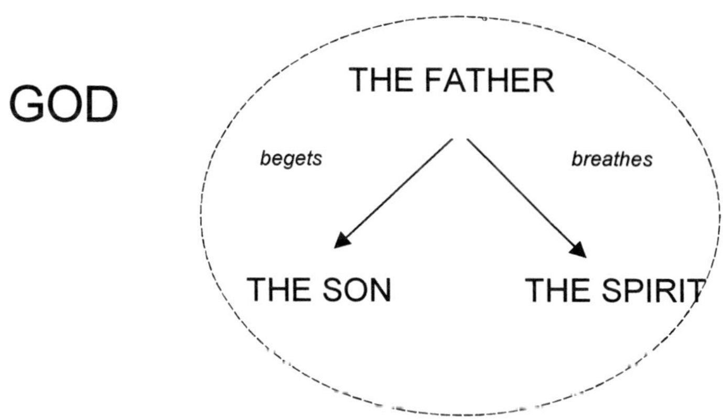

63 Acknowledgment to A.E. McGrath, *Christian Theology: An Introduction*, p298

The Trinity from Augustine to the Reformation

In the Middle Ages in the West there was little change from the Augustinian definitions. Mackey notes that Thomas Aquinas systemised the inherited tradition and did not change it except for the interests of consistency or clarity. Aquinas defines the Persons in terms of 'processions' from each other and relations with each other. The Trinity is self-sufficient and self-contained, with little relation to creation. There is the particular problem of distinguishing the Holy Spirit as a separate Person. Mackey comments:

> Various attributes of the one God which are somehow perceivable to us from his creation can be appropriated to one or other of the persons, and thereby help us to express our belief in the Trinity, but the very use of the term 'appropriation' advertises the fact that nothing in the visible creation is proper to one person rather than to the others … One finds Aquinas honestly admitting that there are no proper names for the procession which results in the Holy Spirit, for the relationship in which it stands to others, or for its 'person', yet striving manfully to show that Love is a proper name for the Holy Spirit, and that Gift is a proper name for the Holy Spirit, when taken personally.[64]

Luther and Calvin, despite their disagreements with Rome, accepted the Roman Catholic doctrine of the Trinity without question. Calvin was a vehement supporter of the Trinity, and supported the execution of the anti-trinitarian Servetus. Luther's theology of the 'Crucified God' had to await further development by Moltmann[65].

Modern theologians and the Trinity

Many modern theologians have recognised that the traditional classical Trinity no longer serves a useful purpose, and the doctrine of the Trinity needs to be re-interpreted or revised. Various ways in which different theologians have re-interpreted the doctrine include:

1. *Reinterpreting the Trinity in terms of experience of God*
2. *Reintroducing the 'economic' Trinity*
3. *Reinterpreting the Trinity in existential terms*
4. *Reinterpretation of the Trinity in terms of a 'social' Trinity*

---

64 J.P. Mackey, *The Christian Experience of God as Trinity*, pp182f.

65 J. Moltmann, The Trinity and the Kingdom of God, 1981. Summarised in J.P. Mackey, in *A New Dictionary of Christian Theology*, pp587f.

5. Reinterpretation of the Trinity towards modalism.

6. Rejection of the Trinity completely

A representative of the first view that the Trinity needs to be understood in terms of experience is the scholar and Anglican bishop J.A.T. Robinson. He wrote in 1967 that:

> Originally the [Trinity] doctrine was created to describe, define and safeguard an experience. But in the process the experience seems to have drained out of it ... we are left with a shell on our hands from which the life that shaped it has long since departed ... And these are the realities which the doctrine of the Trinity attempts to co-ordinate and hold together – namely 'the grace of our Lord Jesus Christ, the love of God, and the fellowship of the Holy Ghost'. [66]

On this view, all that the Christian needs to know about a Trinity is that, somehow, he has met God in Christ, and that this knowledge is made a reality by the presence of the Holy Spirit in the believer and in the Church.

Other theologians have attempted to redefine the classical Trinity in terms of the older ideas of the 'economic' Trinity. J.P. Mackey, in *The Dictionary of Christian Theology*, suggests that the classical, 'essential' Trinity actually *needs* the 'economic' Trinity[67]. The 'Persons' cannot be understood in isolation from subordination of the Son and the Spirit to the Father and their roles in the economy of salvation.[xxxii]

The approach of Karl Barth is more in the direction of modalism. He emphasized the importance of God's self-revelation in the doctrine of the Trinity. The starting point is God's speaking and God's being heard. McGrath summarises:

> ... this might seem to suggest that Barth is really some kind of modalist, treating the different moments of revelation as different 'modes of being' of the same God. It must be conceded that there are those who charge him with precisely this deficiency. Nevertheless, more considered reflection perhaps moves us away from this judgement, although other criticisms can certainly be made. For example, the Spirit fares rather badly in Barth's

---

[66] J.A.T. Robinson, *But That I Can't Believe*, pp87-88.

[67] J.P.Mackey, in *A New Dictionary of Christian Theology*, p588.

> exposition, which in this respect can be argued to mirror weaknesses in the western tradition as a whole[68]

Karl Rahner and Jurgen Moltmann are noted for their efforts to reunite the older 'economic' Trinity with the immanent, 'essential' Trinity. For Rahner

> The 'economic' Trinity is the 'immanent' Trinity, and the 'immanent' Trinity is the 'economic' Trinity. In other words, the way God is revealed and experienced in history corresponds to the way in which God actually is[69]

Moltmann attempted to develop a 'social' doctrine of the Trinity, starting with the conviction that there are really three distinct, though inseparable, divine beings. He makes heavy use of the principle of *perichoresis* ('mutual interpenetration') to try to secure their unity. Mackey notes:

> It must be said that its case for the 'reality' of three distinct pre-existent divine persons is constructed on very shaky exegetical foundations, and its case for the unity of the Godhead involves the very risky manoeuvre of making central to trinitarian argument a concept (*perichoresis*) which in patristic theology is ... peripheral, while ignoring the persistent criticism of this social model.[70]

John Macquarrie considers, like John Robinson, that the definitions of the classical Trinity are no longer relevant today. He proposes an existentialist reinterpretation:

> the trinitarian formula is meant to safeguard the insights of a God who embraces diversity in unity, who is both transcendent and immanent; who is dynamic and yet has stability ... But while these remarks may to some extend defend the traditional doctrine of the Trinity, it will be said that the formula of one substance and three persons constitutes an interpretation that has ceased to communicate, for it talks the language and moves in the universe and discourse of an obsolete philosophy[71]

Macquarrie suggests the Trinity should be expounded in terms of *Being* (taking the idea from Thomas Aquinas, who stated that in God, essence and being are identical). The Father is to be understood as *primordial Being*, the Son as *expressive Being* and the Spirit as *expressive Being*. He concludes that the language of

---

68 A.E. McGrath, *Christian Theology: An Introduction*, p308.

69 A.E. McGrath, *Christian Theology: An Introduction*, p309.

70 J.P. Mackey, in *A New Dictionary of Christian Theology* p588.

71 J. Macquarrie, *Principles of Christian Theology*, p192.

'persons' is unsatisfactory, and that we would do better to think of 'movements' or 'modes' of Being (provided that they are not temporary modes).

Rowan Williams, Archbishop of Canterbury, also seems reluctant to hold to the formulas of the classical Trinity as a statement of final truth. He writes in *Trinity and Ontology*:

> If then, we are serious about the constitutive character of God's relations to Jesus, we are saying that we speak and cannot but speak of God in the context of *limit* - the limits of particularity... of creatureliness. For Jesus is also a creature who prays to God, someone addressing a Father in heaven ... The God who is the ground and form of Jesus' particular history is also the God who calls through the mortal darkness of Gethsemane and Calvary ... It is this that compels us to the trinitarian enterprise; not to find a resolution for all this, but to continue with the question of what is to be said of God, to find a language for the proclaiming of Christ that does not break down into nonsense or presage retreat into abstract theism.[72]

If the definitions of the classical Trinity are 'abstract theism', then Williams is arguing that we should not 'retreat' into them. He talks in his essay *Trinity and Revelation* on recognising the 'absurdity' that Jesus 'is' the creator of the world, and he is at pains to emphasize the authentic humanity of Jesus. Although God, he was 'God as dependent'[73]. Although Williams recognises some of the problems of the 'essential' or 'immanent' Trinity, he will not dismiss it, saying that it is needed to make the life, death and resurrection of Jesus possible and intelligible. But he is also aware of the danger of 'projecting onto God the limits of created identities'[74].

Lampe, in *God as Spirit*, puts forward a spirit-christology which incorporates the idea that *Spirit* and not Word is the key element in the divinity of Jesus, and that the term 'spirit' cannot be restricted to a third, or any, element within divinity. He notes, for example, that Paul seems to make no difference between the Spirit on one hand and the risen Christ on the other. For instance Romans 8:9-11 indicates that there is no difference for Paul between 'the Spirit', 'the Spirit of God' and the 'Spirit of Christ'. The 'Spirit' can stand for any relation of God to the world. Lampe summarises:

---

72 Rowan Williams, *Trinity and Ontology*, in *On Christian Theology*, p158.

73 Rowan Williams, *Trinity and Revelation*, in *On Christian Theology*, p140.

74 Rowan Williams, *Trinity and Ontology*, in *On Christian Theology*, p160.

> A Spirit Christology enables us to say that Jesus is authentically human ... in all respects like ourselves except for the fullness and integrity of his commitment to God's calling ... when we speak of God as Spirit we are not referring to a divine mediator ... Yet in fact we need no mediator. It is God himself, disclosed to us and experienced by us as inspiring and indwelling Spirit (or Wisdom or Word), who meets us through Jesus and can make us Christlike[75]

Mackey comments:

> (Lampe's Christology removes) Christian theology of any alleged need to think in terms of a pre-existent divine person who is distinct from both Father and Spirit, who is called 'Son' or Word', who took human flesh as Jesus of Nazareth ... We should then be left with the God whom Jesus called Father, with this God as Spirit, and with Jesus. We should suffer no theological loss thereby ... since an expanded theology of Spirit would more than compensate for an incarnational theology of questionable pedigree and obsolescent features.[76]

Modern times have also seen outright opposition to the Trinity expressed in theological form. Opposition has come from two main sources, oneness pentecostalism and biblical unitarianism, following respectively the modalist and dynamic monarchian opposition to the Trinity in the second century.

David Bernard, a minister in the United Pentecostal Church, in *The Oneness of God* sets out a oneness pentecostal view. He denies the Trinity, emphasizes the unity of God and affirms the deity of Jesus Christ. He argues that the distinction between 'Father' and 'Son' is accounted for by identifying 'the Father' with God transcendent and 'the Son' with God immanent, and that Jesus' prayer was from an authentic man to God, not from one divine 'Person' to another. In recent years, Bernard has been willing to debate publicly with trinitarian ministers and scholars. While arguing against the Trinity on biblical grounds, Bernard has shown willingness to seek common ground between oneness and trinitarian views, perhaps along the lines of finding some mutually acceptable definition of 'Person'.

Graeser, Lynn and Schoenheit, in *One God and One Lord* represent the biblical unitarian view that Jesus was an anointed man. They argue against the Trinity on both logical and biblical grounds, and they reject the 'God-man' idea of the

---

75 G. Lampe, *God as Spirit*, p144.

76 J.P. Mackey, *The Christian Experience of God as Trinity*, p67.

Incarnation as incoherent. They interpret scriptural texts that have been used to justify the divinity of Jesus in terms of Jesus' divine mission to show God to the world.

Conclusions

The survey has indicated that the doctrine of the Trinity was not present in the church of the 1st century, but was developed during the following three hundred years as theologians tried to reconcile the three principles:

- **The unity of God**
- **The deity of Jesus Christ**
- **The distinction between Father and Son shown in the New Testament**

During this period there was heated debate, and claims and counter claims of heresy, before the doctrine of the Trinity was established in AD 381. There was a strong influence from Greek philosophical thought and perhaps also from wider paganism.

For the Apologists, the term 'The Father' moves away from biblical use as reference to Almighty God and becomes, under influence from Greek philosophy, to mean something like the Platonic Supreme God or Idea, removed from the world and unknowable. This remote Being now needs mediators, both for creation of the world and intervention within it. For the Apologists, this mediator was the divine Logos.

The binitarianism of the Apologists attempted to account for the distinction between Father and Son by sacrificing the unity of God and their subordinationism placed a question mark against the full deity of Christ. The effect of the Logos theology on the idea of 'the Son' was equally significant. The Logos now was a person, whose individuality is derived from the historic Christ. This was projected back on to the historic Christ to give the figure of a divine-human Saviour, with two identities, possibly two sets of memories, consciousnesses and wills (see Chapter 5).

The modalist revolt against the Logos/Eternal Son doctrine attempted to protect the unity of God and the deity of Christ, but at the expense of putting into question the distinction between Father and Son. The modalists asserted that 'Father', 'Son' and 'Spirit' referred to the same person. It seems that the modalists claimed 'Father' and 'Spirit' are practically identical in meaning, whereas 'Son' refers to the humanity of Christ, with the deity of Christ identified as 'the Father', or as the indwelling Spirit.

The first trinitarians, Tertullian, Hippolytus, Clement and Origen tried to reconcile the unity of God and the deity of Christ with the distinction between Father and Son by the use of a 'three-in-one' formula: one substance or essence and three persons. The unity of God becomes again most at risk, because the trinitarians inherited the subordinationism of the Apologists. The three 'persons' were by no means equal. The Son and the Spirit were clearly secondary to the Father, and derived their being from him. This is most clear in the thought of Origen, who talked about the Logos as a 'second God'.

Arianism took the subordinationism of Tertullian and Origen to its logical conclusion, maintaining the unity of God and the Father/Son distinction at the expense of the full deity of Christ. Christ, though supposedly divine, was a created being who was neither God nor man. Arianism was eventually defeated, at least in the official history of Church Councils, by a formula that emphasized the common nature of the Father and the Son in an attempt to safeguard the deity of the Son.

The Constantinople formula establishing the Trinity used the definition of one nature (*ousia*) and three persons (*hypostases*). Under the threat of Arianism, Athanasius and the Cappadocians were obliged to emphasize the same nature and equality of the three persons. For the first time the Holy Spirit was admitted into the Godhead as a divine Person in its own right. The subordinationism of the Apologists and the early trinitarians concerning the Logos being generated from the Father has been replaced by formulas concerning three co-equal and co-eternal Persons. The unity of God and the deity of Christ are (supposedly) safeguarded by the *one nature - three persons* formula. The distinction between Father and Son is (supposedly) accounted for by the distinction between the persons within the Godhead.

The Nicene-Constantinople formula was not the end of the disagreements but the beginning of new problems:

1) The problem of how to account for the distinctions and relations between the Persons, especially in a way that is consistent with the biblical distinction between Father and Son

2) The suspicion of tritheism

For the Cappadocians, and the Eastern tradition, the Father is still regarded as the source of the Godhead. The Father *begets* the Son and *breathes* the Spirit, or the Spirit *proceeds from* the Father. In the West, Augustine formulated the idea of the double procession, whereby the Spirit proceeds from the Father *and* the Son. This attempted to provide a defence against the charge of tritheism, by including the Son within the source of divinity, provided that some explanation could now be given for the existence and role of the Holy Spirit.

With Augustine's Trinity, the gulf between the human Jesus and the eternal Word grew wide. The older subordinationist idea of the Trinity could accommodate the biblical subordination of Christ to God. The new view of absolute equality and Father and Son could not do this. It became problematic how to account for Jesus' ignorance and suffering. Augustine's explanation of the role of the Holy Spirit lacks some credibility. As with the Son, there is a gap between the biblical truth and the theological formula

From Augustine onwards, the Western theological understanding of the Trinity diverged from the Eastern. This division was formalised by the split over the *filioque* clause in the Western creeds, and remains to this day. The Eastern tradition is characterised by a greater acceptance of the separateness of the 'Persons' of the Trinity, and, consequently, a greater vulnerability to the accusation of tritheism. The Western tradition, following Augustine, has a greater emphasis on the unity of the Godhead and the co-equality of the 'Persons'.

A problem for the Western tradition is to reconcile relations between co-equal divine Persons with the subordination of 'the Son' and 'the Spirit' to 'God the Father' shown in the Bible.

Another problem is how the Persons of an 'essential' Trinity could keep their distinctive identities while being an essential unity. Following Augustine, the principles of *perichoresis*, *appropriation* and *opera ad extra sunt indivisa* were devised to do this.

The doctrine of the classical Trinity is now remote from the biblical record of the real-life Son of God and His relationship with His heavenly Father, and also remote from the early ideas of an 'economic' Trinity. In an 'economic' Trinity, where the Persons are defined by their roles in the 'economy' of salvation and there is subordination of the Son and the Spirit to the Father, had some connection with the Bible. The classical Trinity has difficulty in accounting for Jesus' ignorance and his suffering, and his relationship with the Father.

The answer which a Western trinitarian generally gives to the problem of how to account for Jesus' ignorance, suffering and prayer is to talk of the Incarnation. As Jesus was both God and man, his human nature was subject to imperfection and suffering, but his divine nature as the eternal Word remained perfect.[77]

Trinitarian theology since the fifth century has therefore been subject to great tensions and problems. The issue of whether the Trinity leads to tritheism, belief in three gods, has persisted in both traditions. The Eastern tradition emphasized more than the West the distinction between the Persons, and so the West has tended to accuse the East of tritheism. However implicit tritheism is also an issue in the West, where theologians have struggled to define the relations between the persons in various different ways.

The doctrine of the Trinity in the West has other problems, such as how to define an 'essential' Trinity in a way that is compatible with the Bible and avoids a view of Christ as some kind of 'second God'. How can the Son be fully God when the Bible clearly shows him to be subordinate to the Father?

For both Western and Eastern traditions, the Trinity doctrine has always been a barrier to the understanding of Christianity by other religions. In particular, Judaism and Islam see Christianity as violating the monotheism of their sacred scriptures.

[77] See Chapter 5. Note that it is the Incarnation that is being used to explain the Trinity, not the Trinity explaining the Incarnation.

The box summarises the difficulties for the Trinity since the fifth century.

Difficulties for the Trinity doctrine since the fifth century

- **Seen as close to tritheism**
- **Problems distinguishing between the 'Persons'**
- **Problems avoiding Arian view of Christ as 'second God'**
- **Seen by Judaism and Islam as violating monotheism**

Modern theological views have shown scepticism towards the classical Trinity, a willingness to re-interpret the doctrine and an openness to alternative views. However any such willingness to re-interpret the Trinity on the part of theologians has not been reflected in popular understanding. Popular teaching and writing remains rooted in the classical Trinity of three 'Persons'.

Modern developments in the theology of the Trinity

- **scepticism towards the classical Trinity**
- **openness to alternative views**

3. IS THE TRINITY IN THE BIBLE?

The doctrine of the Trinity cannot be found in the Bible

Texts about 'Father. Son and Holy Spirit' do not show God is three 'Persons' but that the one God is revealed through Christ and the Spirit

Finding the Trinity in the Bible

It is well known that the Bible does not include the word 'Trinity', nor does it contain any statement such as 'God is three persons' (or indeed that God is three of anything). Nevetheless trinitarian argument cites much evidence for a Trinity in both Old and New Testaments.

This chapter and the next three chapters discuss the biblical evidence for a Trinity (see box). The Old Testament evidence is considered first. The main evidence from the New Testament is then outlined and key 'trinitarian' texts are examined. The following three chapters discuss the specific evidence for the 'God the Father', 'God the Son' and 'God the Spirit'. In all cases it is concluded that the Bible does not show a Trinity.

The main types of evidence for the Trinity in the Bible

- **Old Testament texts suggesting God is plural**
- **OT texts suggesting pre-existence of Christ**
- **New Testament texts suggesting God is three persons**
- **NT texts showing 'the Son' separate from 'the Father'**
- **NT texts suggesting 'the Spirit' separate from 'the Father'**

Old Testament evidence for a Trinity

A common cause of difference between Jews and Christians is over whether God is *singular* (one person) or *plural* (more than one person). It is frequently said that Jews believe God to be singular whereas trinitarians read the Old Testament in the light of the New Testament and find evidence for the plurality of God (see box).

> Old Testament evidence for the plurality of God
>
> - **God's activity in creation shows God is plural**
> - **Plural pronouns in e.g. 'Let us make man'**
> - **Plurality of the name *Elohim***
> - **Three visitors to Abraham in Genesis 18**
> - **'Personifications' of the pre-existent Christ and the Spirit**
> - **Prophetic references to 'the Son' indicating pre-existence**
> - **God appearing to talk amongst himself**

Most Jews emphatically believe God to be singular because of the singularity of the Hebrew name for God and because of the most important statement of belief in Judaism, the *Shema*:

The Lord our God is **one** *Lord (Deuteronomy 6:4)*

Trinitarians would read this verse either as asserting monotheism, that there is only one God, or else as saying that the three Persons of the Trinity form a composite unity in association together. Non-trinitarians would interpret it according to its literal meaning as saying that God is singular.

In Judaism, God reveals himself as the self-existent one; the only being that can exist without qualification or dependence on other beings. The Hebrew verb *Havah* ('to be') is used for the name that most describes his nature:

God said unto Moses, I AM THAT I AM: and he said, Thus shalt thou say unto the children of Israel, I AM hath sent me unto you (Exodus 3:14)

The Hebrew name for God is Jehovah or Yahweh, translated LORD in the KJV. This means literally HE IS. There is no suggestion of plurality in the language used.

Trinitarians tend to ignore this fundamental evidence for the singularity of God and try to find evidence for plurality in other parts of scripture.

Genesis 1:1-3

Genesis Chapter 1 is often cited as a source for the Trinity. God's activity in creation described in Genesis 1:1-3 is seen as the work of Father, Son and Spirit. However the passage in Genesis 1:1-3 does not imply plurality in God. Verse 1 mentions God in a singular way as being responsible for creation, with no mention of plurality of divine persons being involved.

Verse 2 talks about 'the spirit of God' moving on the face of the waters. Yet there is no implication that there is a separate divine person involved. There is no evidence in verse 2 that the spirit of God is a separate person from some other person called 'the Father'.

Verse 3 states that 'God said ...'. Again there is no implication that there is any separate person here called the Word of God. To speak about 'the Word of God' does not imply a personality for the Word of God separate from God or from some supposed First Person, any more than to speak of 'the word of John' means that John's word has some independent personality of its own.

A trinitarian may reply that, nevertheless, the text shows God active in a threefold way. This is correct, but it does not imply that God's activity and self-revelation is as three 'Persons'. The first act, that of creation, is that of *God himself*, not some 'First Person'. The actions by God's Word and Spirit are never shown in scripture as belonging to two pre-existent 'Persons' of the Godhead, but as actions of *God himself* acting in two different personal ways.

Plural pronouns for God

Trinitarian argument makes heavy use of four instances in the Old Testament where the plural personal pronouns 'we' and 'us' are used for God. In all instances God is speaking:

'Let us make man in our image' (Genesis 1:26)

'Behold the man is become as one of us' (Genesis 3:22)

'Let us go down, and there confound their language' (Genesis 11:7)

'Whom shall I send, and who will go for us?' (Isaiah 6:8)

In reply to this, a king or other royalty may refer to himself as 'we' using the so-called 'plural of majesty'. When a king says 'we', he refers to himself as embodying the whole plurality of royal attributes, but not as more than one personality. The plural of majesty is used in the Bible by King Artaxerxes in Ezra 4:18.

God may talk about himself in the plural in this way, without implying that he is more than one person. A verse like 'Let *us* make man' does not prove that God is plural, any more than a king talking about 'we' or 'us' indicates that he is composed of more than one person. The plural of majesty can explain all of these passages.[xxxiii]

Plural pronouns for God occur very rarely in the Old Testament, and are greatly outnumbered by the singular pronouns 'I', 'me' and 'myself'. Singular pronouns for God are used 7,742 times in the Old Testament. If God is a Trinity, how can the trinitarian explain why plural pronouns occur so rarely but singular pronouns so frequently? As an example of singular pronouns, consider Isaiah 44:24:

Thus saith the Lord, thy redeemer, and he that formed thee from the womb.

I am the Lord that maketh all things: that stretcheth forth the heavens alone:

that spreadeth abroad the earth by myself (Isaiah 44:24)

The difficulty for a trinitarian interpretation of this verse is to be able to say who is talking when God is recorded as speaking. Is it 'God the Father' talking, or is it the whole Trinity?[78] If it is the 'God the Father' talking, then this excludes the other two and the implication is that the Son and the Spirit are other than God. If it is the whole Trinity talking, then it should read '*We* are the Lord'. But the phrases 'We are the Lord' and 'We are God' are *never* used in the Old Testament, whereas 'I am God' or 'I am the Lord' are used a total of 493 times.[79]

---

[78] See Chapter 4 for discussion on the problem of identifying the voice of 'The Father'.

[79] e.g. Isaiah 45:8 and 22. Figures from Strong's Concordance and Blue LetterBible.

The plurality of *Elohim*

Some trinitarians cite the fact that the name *Elohim* for God (translated as 'God' in the KJV) is a plural noun. *Elohim* is used to refer to God about 2300 times[xxxiv]. The entry in Strong's Concordance reads:

> plural of *eloah* (a god); *gods* in the ordinary sense; but specially used of the supreme *God* ...

Some trinitarians would use the fact that *Elohim* is a plural form as evidence for the Trinity. But this is a weak point to make, given the general hostility of Jews to the idea of plurality of God and the fact that *Elohim* is so frequently used in the Old Testament. It is difficult to understand how could Jews accept such a word for God so frequently if they understood to imply that God is plural. In fact the plurality of *Elohim* when used in reference to Jehovah is commonly understood by Jews as representing the plurality of the *attributes* of God.

It is significant that trinitarian attempts to find a Trinity in the Old Testament do not put much weight on the plural meaning of *Elohim*. For instance Bowman, in *The Biblical Basis of the Doctrine of the Trinity*, acknowledges that:

> the 'plural of amplitude' or of 'fullness' probably does explain the use of the plural form *elohim* in the singular sense of 'God'[80]

Appearance of three men to Abraham

The appearance of God ('theophany') to Abraham in the form of three men in Genesis 18 is often taken to be evidence of the Trinity. However God may appear to men in any form that he chooses, whether it be as one man, two men, three men or a voice speaking from a burning bush. The number of 'men' is irrelevant.

Furthermore the evidence indicates that at least two of the men were not an appearance of God at all, but angels. Verse 22 states that the men left and went towards Sodom 'but Abraham stood yet before the Lord'. The following chapter describes two *angels* arriving at Sodom. A natural conclusion might be that, of the original three 'men', one was a theophany and the other two were angels. But there is not enough evidence in the passage for any firm conclusions.

---

80 Bowman, *The Biblical Basis of the Doctrine of the Trinity*, p5.

Personification of attributes of God

A text that is frequently used to justify the pre-existence of Christ is the poem about wisdom in Proverbs 8. Christ is identified with the Wisdom of God, and a verse like 'The Lord possessed me at the beginning of his way …' (Proverbs 8:22) is used to justify the claim that Christ existed in the beginning. References to an attribute of God in a personal way, known as 'personification of intermediaries' is a common literary device in the Old Testament. It is incorrect to conclude that these attributes of God correspond to separate personalities.

Consider the Wisdom of God. The references to Wisdom in Proverbs 8 are often taken as referring to a pre-existent 'God the Son', but there is no implication of an independent personality. Wisdom is an attribute of God, and it is related to the Word (*logos*) of God. Viewed like this, the pre-existence of Wisdom (Proverbs 8:22-231) is a parallel passage to John 1:1-2. The Wisdom and the Word, as attributes of God, were involved in creation. For example:

By the word of the Lord were the heavens made: and all the host of them by the breath of his mouth (Psalm 33:6)

To him that by wisdom made the heavens: for his mercy endureth for ever (Psalm 136:5)

These passages and many like them refer to attributes of God using poetic language, and cannot be interpreted literally. Should one believe that God created literally by the breath of His mouth? Does God have a literal mouth? These passages do not mean that God's Wisdom or His Word were there alongside God as separate entities, any more than Psalm 136:5 implies that God's mercy somehow sits next to God on His throne, enduring ever. The passages describe God's activity in creation using poetic language. They do not imply separate personalities for each attribute mentioned.

There is therefore no reason why Proverbs 8 should be interpreted as implying that there is a divine person called 'Wisdom' who co-exists with other divine persons in the Godhead.

There is another problems with identifying the 'God the Son' of the Trinity with the 'Wisdom' of Proverbs 8. Proverbs 8:22 refers to the creation of Wisdom at the beginning of God's work. If Wisdom can be identified as 'God the Son', then God the Son is a created being and the first of all creation. The idea that the Son is a created being is the Arian view, which the doctrine of the Trinity was formulated to oppose and which has been condemned as heretical since AD 381.

The theologian Geoffrey Lampe, in the 1976 Bampton Lectures, describes the use of terms like 'Word', 'Wisdom' and 'Spirit' in the Old Testament as 'bridge' terms, which express the idea of God' relationship with creation. He includes in this category other terms such as the 'arm', 'finger', 'hand', 'power', 'face' and 'angel of God'. He writes:

> These terms are not predicated directly and immediately of God. In their original and proper usage they are not descriptive of the being of God. They are, rather, attempts to describe certain aspects of man's awareness of God, and when these concepts, which are drawn from the experience of encounter between human beings, are used for that purpose they are applied to God by analogy. Such words as 'Word', Wisdom', and 'Spirit' are quasi-poetical words ... In their original usage they are not metaphysical terms, descriptive of deity itself; nor do they denote hypostatically existent mediators between God and the world[81]

'Wisdom', 'Word' and 'Spirit' can each be described as having personal characteristics. However this usage in the Old Testament does not support the classical Trinity of three co-existent divine persons. The fact that God's Wisdom, Word, Name and Spirit are described in personal terms when they show God in action does not make them independent personalities within the Godhead.

Prophetic references to the Messiah or the 'Son of Man'

Do the prophetic references to the Messiah as *Son* or *Lord* in the Old Testament indicate plurality in God? Emphatically not. These passages do not suggest that person talked about, 'the Son', was a divine person. Most scholars agree that they refer to the ideal king of David's line, who came to be known as the Messiah, the anointed one, exercising delegated authority, and clearly subject to God. Such a person has to be a man.

Old Testament texts typically refer to the Messiah in terms of *subordination to God* and *anointing by God*. Two such, much quoted in the New Testament, are:

The LORD hath said unto me, Thou art my Son; this day have I begotten thee (Psalm 2:7)

The LORD said unto my Lord, Sit thou at my right hand, until I make thine enemies thy footstool (Psalm 110:1) [xxxv]

---

[81] G. Lampe, *God as Spirit*, p37.

To take prophecies of the Messiah as proof of the existence of a 'God the Son' would be completely contradictory to the meaning and context of these passages.

A trinitarian might take reference to 'the Son of Man' in Daniel 7 as proof of a second divine figure beside a 'God the Father'. This was of course the title that Jesus used to refer to himself. However the 'Son of Man' is clearly a man. In Daniel 7 he is contrasted with the 'Ancient of Days' and is clearly subordinate to him. If this 'Son of Man' is a divine figure, it could not be the co-equal 'God the Son' of the Trinity, but a second rank divinity. Besides, the natural way to understand 'the Ancient of Days' is as a reference to God himself, not a First Person of a Trinity.

Isaiah 48:16

Trinitarian argument often singles out Isaiah 48:16:

Come ye near unto me, hear ye this; I have not spoken in secret from the beginning; from the time that it was, there am I: and now the Lord God, and his Spirit, hath sent me

The context is a collection of prophecies concerning Israel and Cyrus. Some translations put the preceding passage in quotes, and leave this statement out of quotes. A trinitarian would read it as the 'God the Son' talking. It is important for trinitarians because it is one of the very few passages in the Old Testament where the voice of the 'God the Son' is supposedly heard.

However we notice that the speaker and the Spirit are both sent by '*the Lord God*', and 'Lord' refers, as it usually does, to Yahweh. The sender is *God himself*, not a 'God the Father'. We can readily understand the speaker to be a literary personification of the divine Word of God, similar to Wisdom in Proverbs 8, and then see the passage as describing the sending of the Word and the Spirit by God.

Note that there is no reference by the speaker to being the Son of God. If the speaker were Jesus, the Son of God, then the statement would be false, because Jesus had not been sent at the time of writing. God sent the Son when Jesus was born.

Other supposed references to plurality in God

Most trinitarians would say that the Jews wrongly believe God is singular. However some say that plurality in God was always there in the Jewish faith. For instance Simon Hawthorne, in an essay *Three in the Holy One of Israel*[82] published by the Centre for Biblical and Hebraic Studies, claims that in Judaism the Word (Aramaic 'Memra') of God and the Name of God were considered sometimes to act as God and to be worshipped as God[xxxvi]. This 'personification of intermediaries' in the Old Testament has already been discussed. It does not prove the Word and the Name of God are separate personalities in the Godhead.

A different attempt to find multiple personality in God refers to texts talking of angels. Hawthorne cites the 'Metatron', the highest archangel of Judaism. The Metatron is cited in rabbinic commentaries (some of them written hundreds of years after Christ) as the angel who wrestled with Jacob, one who occupies the throne next to God, the link between the human and the divine, and the Middle Pillar (in the Godhead), Lord and Messenger[83]. However powerful an angel may be, he is still only an angel. Angels are created beings, which the trinitarian Persons cannot be. The Son cannot be an angel, as he is 'so much better than the angels' (Hebrews 1:4). The trinitarian attempt to prove that God is plural by citing rabbinic texts about the Metatron is self-defeating (on trinitarian terms) because it reintroduces the Arian idea that Jesus is a created being.

Because God speaks as 'I' so many times in the Old Testament, and only a few times as 'we', the trinitarian must claim that the three persons of the Trinity generally speak in unison. The many times that God talks of himself in singular terms ('I am God alone', 'I am one Lord' etc.)[xxxvii] have to be interpreted in trinitarian terms as the whole Trinity speaking with one voice. But then why does the Bible not say '*We* are the Lord' etc.? The trinitarian has no real answer to this, other than to say that the plurality of God is made clear in the New Testament[84]. As we shall see, this is not so.

In conclusion the overwhelming evidence from the Old Testament is that God is *singular* and not plural. This is how most Jews understand their scriptures. The few instances of plural pronouns can be explained by the plural of majesty.

---

[82] J. Fieldsend et al (1998), *Roots and Branches*.

[83] Hawthorne quotes Rabbis Simeon ben Jochai and Bechai, Fieldsend et al (1998), p170.

[84] See Chapter 4 for the problems of identifying the voice of 'the Father'.

New Testament evidence for a Trinity

The trinitarian claim is that the New Testament shows God to be a Trinity of three 'Persons', Father, Son and Spirit. This claim is highly problematic.

There are three main weaknesses with the attempt to prove a Trinity from scripture. These are:

1. There is no trinitarian 'First Person' in the New Testament. All texts that supposedly show a 'First Person' actually refer to God himself (see Chapter 4).

2. There is no trinitarian 'Second Person' in the New Testament. All texts that supposedly show a 'Second Person' actually refer to Jesus Christ *the man*, not to a pre-existent Eternal Son. This is true even when the ascended Christ is described as at the right hand of the Father (see Chapter 5).

3. There is a complete lack of scriptural evidence for the Holy Spirit as a separate personality within the Godhead (see Chapter 6).

There is no statement anywhere in the New Testament of a supposed 'threeness' of God except 1 John 5:7 (KJV):

For there are three that bear record in heaven, the Father, the Word and the Holy Ghost: and these three are one (1 John 5:7)

However this verse does not appear in any early manuscripts and is agreed by scholars to be a later addition. The Blue Letter Bible comments that 'It is probably best to regard the insertion as the efforts of an over-zealous copyist who thought that the New Testament needed a little help with the doctrine of the Trinity'[85]. The example of 1 John 5:7 shows that later editors or transcribers were seemingly quite willing to give a trinitarian 'gloss' to New Testament scriptures. The same might have happened with other verses (see discussion of Matthew 28:19 below).

When Jesus in Mark 12:29 was asked what was the first commandment, he repeated the *Shema*: "Hear O Israel, the Lord our God is one Lord". If Jesus had intended to bring a new trinitarian insight to the concept of God, he could have 'updated' the Shema by saying: "The Lord our God is one Lord, but He is really three". But he did not.

The case for seeing a Trinity in the New Testament is put by Alister McGrath:

---

[85] www.blueletterbible.org

> The casual reader of Scripture will discern a mere two verses in the entire Bible which seem ... to be capable of a trinitarian interpretation: Matthew 28:19 and 2 Corinthians 13:13 (sic). Both these verses have become deeply rooted in the Christian consciousness, the former on account of its baptismal associations, and the latter through the common use of the formula in Christian prayer and devotion. Yet these two verses ... can hardly be thought of as constituting a doctrine of the Trinity. Happily, the ultimate grounds of the doctrine are not to be sought exclusively in these two verses. Rather, the foundations of the doctrine of the Trinity are to be found in the pervasive pattern of divine activity to which the New Testament bears witness. The Father is revealed in Christ through the Spirit.[86]

Trinitarians cite scriptural texts to support this theme of a trinitarian 'pervasive pattern of divine activity', mainly to be found in the Gospel of John, Ephesians, Philippians, Colossians and Hebrews. In the synoptic gospels there are texts used to support plurality in God, notably the baptism of Jesus and the 'baptism formula' of Matthew 28:19. The trinitarian E. Calvin Beisner[87], in the John Ankerberg debate, said that his belief in the Trinity rested on such passages.

Main evidence for the Trinity in the New Testament

- **God described as three 'Persons': Father, Son and Spirit**
- **'The Son' seemingly separate from 'the Father'**
- **'The Son' seemingly pre-existent**
- **'The Son' seemingly involved in Creation**
- **'The Son' described as at the right hand of 'the Father'**
- **'The Spirit' seemingly a distinct person from 'the Son' and 'the Father'**

We will now examine the texts that are cited to imply that God is three 'Persons', looking first at the Great Commission of Matthew 28:19 and the baptism of Jesus, and then at other 'trinitarian' texts.

---

86 A.E. McGrath, *Christian Theology: An Introduction*, p293. (Presumably 2 Corinthians 3:14 is meant rather than 2 Corinthians 3:13).

87 J. Ankerberg et al, 1985.

The Great Commission of Matthew 28:19

Trinitarians give special prominence to the 'Great Commission' of Jesus in Matthew 28:19:

Go ye therefore, and teach all nations, baptizing them in the name of the Father, and of the Son, and of the Holy Ghost

Trinitarian scholars cite one of the rules of Greek grammar laid down by the Greek grammarian Granville Sharp to argue that this passages shows three distinct persons. The relevant Granville Sharp rule is that when two or more noun descriptors are joined together with the Greek word *kai*, meaning 'and', followed by the definite article 'the', then the things referred to are different from each other. Therefore, trinitarians argue, the Trinity is set out in the words of Jesus.

Three points can be made to refute this. Firstly 'Father', 'Son' and 'Holy Ghost' are titles not names. If the word 'name' used in the text means 'proper name', then the fact it is singular not plural indicates only *one* named object or person. It is recorded in Acts that the apostles baptized in the name of Jesus only ('Jesus Christ' Acts 2:38 and 10:48, 'the Lord Jesus' Acts 8:16, 19:5). There is no recorded instance of baptism using the three titles. It is possible that the text was modified later, and the original was an instruction to baptize in his name only[xxxviii]. Even if Jesus actually said the words as currently stated, his followers did not see that as inconsistent with baptizing in the single name of Jesus.

Alternatively the phrase 'in the name of' when used in the Bible may mean 'on the authority of' rather than 'using the (proper) name of'. The same argument applies, that there is a *single* authority for baptism, which the apostles clearly thought to be that of the Lord Jesus. The apostles did not seem to think that authority from three Persons was needed to baptize a person.

Secondly it cannot be shown conclusively that Granville Sharp's rules applied at the time that Paul was writing[xxxix].

Thirdly even if the words 'the Father, and of the Son, and of the Holy Ghost' are accurately reported of Jesus and were used to indicate three different personal aspects of God, that does not prove that these personal aspects are the same types of 'thing'. Still less does it prove that they are independently co-existing members of a Trinity.

In fact, 'Father' in the New Testament refers to God himself (see Chapter 4), not a 'God the Father'. 'Son' refers to Jesus Christ, the man, the risen Saviour (see Chapter 5). 'Spirit' refers to God in his relationship to humans, not a separate divine person (see Chapter 6). The three titles 'Father', 'Son' and 'Holy Ghost' are distinguishable aspects of God, but they are not three 'Persons' of the same kind of nature.

Finally we should note that these are the last words of Jesus recorded in the Gospel of Matthew. If the trinitarian interpretation is correct, and Jesus' words assume a Trinity, then surely Jesus would have taught on the Trinity before that time. However Jesus is not reported in this gospel (or any other) as teaching a Trinity.

The baptism of Jesus

The baptism of Jesus is often used as evidence for a Trinity.

And Jesus, when he was baptised, went up straightway out of the water: and lo, the heavens were opened unto him, and he saw the Spirit of God descending like a dove, and lighting upon him: and lo a voice from heaven, saying, this is my beloved Son, in whom I am well pleased. (Matt 3:16f cf Luke 3:21f)

The reports of this event describe the Son on earth, the Holy Spirit descending and the voice from heaven. The trinitarian would say that, if the first two are 'God the Son' and 'God the Spirit', then the third must be 'God the Father'.

The first point to make is that the baptism of Jesus has no theological relevance to a Trinity. Although trinitarians teachers often refer to Jesus' baptism as 'proof' of the Trinity, theologians who discuss this event are completely silent about any trinitarian implications. Their focus is on how the descent of the Spirit symbolises the adoption by God of *the man* Jesus as Messiah and how the anointing of the Spirit equips him for ministry.

The public ministry of Jesus, as described in Matthew and Luke, commences with his baptism, followed by the temptations in the wilderness. The baptism is clearly of great symbolic importance. It inaugurates Jesus as the Messiah, bringing in the New Age of the Kingdom of God[xl]. The event is the equivalent of a prophet's call, or anointing from God, which is symbolised by the depiction of the Holy Spirit descending. However the descent of the Holy Spirit cannot be taken entirely literally, because if Jesus were already the Son of God[88], he would already have the Holy Spirit available to Him. What it symbolises is the beginning of the inauguration of the Messianic New Age and the ministry of Jesus, the time from which the Holy Spirit would be available to him in power. This is emphasised in Luke's version, which describes Jesus subsequently as 'led of the Spirit' into the wilderness. Matthew's version records Jesus' words, in answer to John's questioning his baptism, as 'Suffer it to be so now: for thus it becometh us to fulfil all righteousness'. These indicate the symbolism of Jesus' baptism. Its purpose is to show publicly that the mantle of Elijah, inherited by John[89], has passed to Jesus.

The trinitarian interpretation of Jesus baptism is not only unnecessary theologically, but is also full of difficulty. The first problem with the trinitarian interpretation is that the voice from heaven is *God Himself*, not a 'God the Father'. Jesus was the Son of God, so the voice must be that of God. Trinitarians have never been able to distinguish satisfactorily between the voice of God speaking in his whole supposed 'triunity' and the voice of a 'God the Father' (see Chapter 4).

Secondly, if Jesus was 'God the Son' incarnate, he would have been born so. How could he receive 'God the Spirit' in any meaningful sense? As 'God the Son' he would already have all the Godhead anyway, so what more could he receive?

Thirdly, the Holy Spirit is not a 'Third Person' in this scene or in any other in the Bible (see Chapter 6). God is a spirit (John 4:24), and does not need a separate personality to move amongst men.

A voice from heaven with Jesus on earth at the same time does not require two 'divine Persons'. To say that the *appearance* of three implies there must *be* three divine 'Persons' is to confuse categories. The omnipresent God may manifest himself in any way he chooses. The manifestations of the voice of God and the Holy Spirit descending at the baptism of Jesus do not prove a Trinity.

---

88 Luke 1:35.

89 Matthew 17:12, Mark 9:13.

Other 'trinitarian' texts

Robert Bowman, in *The Biblical Basis of the Doctrine of the* Trinity, cites fifty four New Testament texts in support of the Trinity. He states:

> The New Testament presents a consistent triad of Father, Son, Holy Spirit (God, Christ, Spirit): Matthew 28:19, 2 Corinthians 13:14 also *(52 texts are cited).* Therefore the Bible does teach a Trinity[xli]

Nicky Gumbel in *Is the Trinity Unbiblical Unbelievable and Irrelevant?* says of Matthew 28:19 and 2 Corinthians 13:14 that:

> ... while these two texts do not expressly state the doctrine of the Trinity, they point towards it. [90]

Do these and other texts point towards a Trinity? Consider first the fact that the texts that supposedly show a Trinity are outnumbered by far by texts in which the two 'Persons' God ('the Father') and Jesus Christ (or 'the Son') are described together *without any reference to the Spirit.* Examples are the salutations and blessings (see Chapter 4) and the numerous occasions where Jesus is described as being at the right hand of God (see Chapter 5).

Taking the example of the salutations, a typical greeting is from 'God our Father and the Lord Jesus Christ'. Although a trinitarian may cite them as evidence for 'the Father' and 'the Son' being separate divine 'Persons' (for this see Chapter 5), the problem here is that *not a single salutation is from the Holy Spirit as well.*

Consider also Paul's Letter to the Colossians. Colossians is an important doctrinal letter and verses 1:13-20 are cited by trinitarians as evidence for the pre-existence of Christ. However Bowman cites no texts from Colossians because there is no mention of the Holy Spirit in the entire letter.

The texts cited by Bowman associate together 'the Father' (or 'God'), 'the Son' (or 'Jesus Christ') and 'the Spirit' in some way. However just because a passage of text mentions God, or 'the Father', Christ, or 'the Son' and the Holy Spirit within a few verses, does not imply that the passage teaches a Trinity. A trinitarian is looking for a statement that relates the activity of the three so-called Persons. Verses like Matthew 28:19, 2 Corinthians 13:14, Ephesians 2:18, 4:4-6, Hebrews 9:14 would appear to come into this category. Although they

---

[90] N. Gumbel, *Is the Trinity Unbiblical Unbelievable and Irrelevant?*, p10.

do not actually teach a Trinity, it is understandable for a trinitarian to see them in that light. Bowman also cites some passages that are hardly 'trinitarian' in this sense. Seven speak of only two of the supposed 'Persons' (for instance Luke 1:35, John 7:37-39, Acts 5:3f, 9f, 2 Corinthians 3:6-8, Ephesians 4:29-32, Hebrews 10:28-31). Eleven texts mention all three 'Persons', but do not seem to attempt to teach a Trinity at all (Luke 4:1-12, John 4:10-25, Acts 1:4-8, 2:33, 2:38f, 7:55f, 10:44-48, 11:15-18, 15:8-11, Galatians 3:8-14, Ephesians 5:18-20).

Consider Luke 4:1-12. In this passage Jesus is described as 'full of the Holy Spirit' and 'led by the Spirit'. Even if one accepts that the 'Son of God' is a pre-existent divine person, the passage only refers to the Spirit as an influence, not a divine person.

John 4:10-25 is another example. This passage talks about the Spirit, the 'living water', as a gift of God. Later Jesus said that 'God is (a) spirit'. Likewise Acts 1:4ff, 2:33, 2:38f, Galatians 3:8-14) refer to the Spirit as a 'promise' and a 'gift'. These passages do not teach that the Spirit has a separate personality from that of 'the Father' and 'the Son'.

If we leave out these eighteen passages, that leaves thirty six remaining. Matthew 28:19 and Luke 3:21f have already been discussed. Of the rest, the following seven appear to make the trinitarian case most strongly:

But when the Comforter is come, whom I shall send unto you from the Father, even the Spirit of truth, which proceedeth from the Father (John 15:26)

But ye are not in the flesh, but in the Spirit, if so be that the Spirit of God dwell in you. Now if any man have not the Spirit of Christ, he is none of his. And if Christ be in you, the body is dead because of sin; but the Spirit is life because of righteousness. But if the Spirit of him that raised up Jesus from the dead dwell in you, he that raised up Christ from the dead shall also quicken your mortal bodies by his Spirit that dwelleth in you (Romans 8:9-11)

Now there are diversities of gifts but the same Spirit. And there are differences of administrations, but the same Lord. And there are diversities of operations, but it is the same God which worketh all in all (1 Corinthians 12:4-6)

The grace of the Lord Jesus Christ and the love of God and the fellowship of the Holy Spirit be with you all (2 Corinthians 13:14)

For through him (Christ) we both have access in one Spirit to the Father (Ephesians 2:18)

There is one body, and one Spirit, even as ye are called in one hope of your calling: one Lord, one faith one baptism, one God and Father of all, who is above all, and through all, and in you all (Ephesians 4:4-6)

Elect according to the foreknowledge of God the Father, through sanctification of the Spirit, unto obedience and sprinkling of the blood of Jesus Christ: Grace to you, and peace, be multiplied (1 Peter 1:2)

Nicky Gumbel, in trying to show that the New Testament teaches a Trinity, comments on Ephesians:

> Paul sees virtually every aspect of the Christian faith and life in trinitarian terms, ... both halves of (Chapter 1) are 'essentially trinitarian ... both are addressed to God the Father ... both refer specifically to God's work in and through Christ ... both sections of the chapter allude ... to the work of the Holy Spirit ... Christian faith and life are both fundamentally trinitarian ...
>
> In Chapter 2 ... our relationship with God and prayer is seen in trinitarian terms. We pray 'to the Father' through Jesus, 'by one spirit' (Ephesians 2:18) ... In Chapter 4 Christian unity is urged for trinitarian reasons: 'There is ... one Spirit ... one Lord ... One God and Father of all' (Ephesians 4:4-6) [91]

Trinitarian interpretation of these texts requires 'the Father' to refer to a 'First Person' and 'the Son' to refer to a 'Second Person'. Both are incorrect. 'The Father' in these texts is just another name for God. In some passages (Ephesians 4:6, 1 Corinthians 12:6) 'God' is used instead of 'the Father' and this makes the reference clear. The 'Father' figure is not a 'First Person' but is God. If 1 Corinthians 12 were describing three divine Persons, then Jesus and the Holy Spirit would be *other than God*, divine beings subordinate to the true God. There is a tendency towards tritheism in trinitarianism because of the difficulties in interpreting texts like these (see Chapter 7).

'The Son' in these texts is never a pre-existent Eternal Son, but always the man Christ Jesus. In the epistles, Jesus is the risen Lord, the begotten Son of God at the right hand of God, but still a man (see Chapter 5).

There is certainly a profound truth behind what trinitarian writers like Bowman, McGrath and Gumbel are saying. However this truth is not that God is three

---

[91] N. Gumbel, *Is the Trinity Unbiblical Unbelievable and Irrelevant?*, pp10-11.

'Persons'. These so-called 'trinitarian' texts show that God is working through Christ and through his Spirit. They do not show Christ as a pre-existent 'Eternal Son', but as the man Christ Jesus, the Son of God, ascended and seated at the right hand of God.

Notice that in the quote above Bowman includes (God, Christ, Spirit) in brackets after 'consistent triad of Father, Son, Holy Spirit', as if these triads are the same. They can only be the same if it is recognised that the correct biblical reference of 'Father' is not some 'First Person' and that it is the risen Christ who is at the right hand of God, not an 'Eternal Son'.

Notice again the weakness of the trinitarian interpretation of these verses in terms of three 'Persons'. For, if the first member of the triad is God (as Bowman actually recognises) then the other two members of the triad must be *other than God.* These texts cannot refer to three divine 'Persons' at all.

Gregory Boyd, in *Oneness Pentecostals and the Trinity*, tries to address this last point and says it was 'literary convention' for New Testament authors to refer to the First Person of the Trinity as 'God'[92]. However Boyd does not give any evidence for this statement. How can we know that Paul, for example, is referring to a First Person of a Trinity when he mentions 'God', in the company of Christ and the Spirit?[93]

In conclusion, the 'trinitarian texts' do not describe three divine 'Persons' at all, but God revealed and active through Jesus Christ and the Holy Spirit. There is no implication in these passages that Jesus and the Holy Spirit are co-equal 'Persons'.

Texts used to support the divinity of Jesus

Numerous passages are commonly cited to support the traditional doctrine of the Incarnation, that Jesus is fully God as well as man. Principal texts are John 1:14, John 20:28 and Colossians 2:9.

---

92 Boyd, *Oneness Pentecostals and the Trinity*, p57.

93 In Chapter 4 there is a more detailed consideration of Boyd's argument.

If Jesus is God, and seemingly a separate person from a 'God the Father', then there seem to be two divine persons. Therefore evidence that Jesus is divine is seen by trinitarians as evidence for a Trinity. This is an incorrect deduction. The fact that God is revealed in Jesus that does not prove that there are two co-eternal divine 'Persons', 'the Father' and 'the Son'. To take one example of alternative belief, oneness pentecostals accept the full divinity of Christ but deny the Trinity completely (see Chapter 5).

Texts suggesting a pre-existent 'Eternal Son'

Texts which are used as evidence for a pre-existent 'Eternal Son' include John 1:1-14, John 6:38, 17:5, Colossians 1:15-19 and 1 John 1:1f. The reasons why they do not show an 'Eternal Son' are briefly:

1. There cannot be a 'Second Person' because there is no 'First Person' (see Chapter 4).

2. A 'Second Person' cannot address a 'First Person' as 'my God', but Jesus addresses God in this way (see Chapter 5).

3. A 'Second Person' cannot pray to a 'First Person', as Jesus prays to God (see Chapter 5).

4. A 'Second Person' cannot be a mediator between humanity and a 'First Person' (see Chapter 5).

5. In the texts cited, pre-existence is either applied to the Word of God (John 1:1) or to the man Christ Jesus, never to an Eternal 'Second Person' (see Chapter 5).

6. In the case of the man Christ Jesus, pre-existence means pre-existence in the plan of God, not actual existence (see Chapter 5).

Texts showing the risen Christ separate from God

The New Testament has numerous references to the risen Lord at the right hand of God. However *none* of them mention the Holy Spirit. If God were a Trinity then we would expect descriptions of three in heaven, or greetings from all three 'Persons'. These cannot be found in the New Testament.

Many texts show the risen Christ at the right hand of God (Matthew 26:64, Mark 14:62, Luke 22:69, Acts 2:33ff, 7:55f, Romans 8:34, 1 Corinthians 15:24ff, Ephesians 1:20, Philippians 2:9, Colossians 3:1, Hebrews 1:3,1:13, 4:14, 7:26, 8:1, 10:12f, 12:2, 1 Peter 3:22, Revelation 5:6f). They do not describe two divine 'Persons' together in heaven, but God and the risen Jesus (see Chapter 5 for further discussion).

The greetings in Paul's epistles are always from Christ and God, not from two divine 'Persons'. A typical example is:

Grace to you and peace from God our Father, and the Lord Jesus Christ (Romans 1:7)

The terms 'God our Father', 'God the Father', and so on, are all used to refer to God himself, and not to a 'First Person' (see Chapter 4).

Other references to God and Christ together are 1 Timothy 5:21, 1 Timothy 6:13, 2 Timothy 4:1, Philippians 4:20, Colossians 1:3 and Hebrews 8:1. These texts do not show the existence of a 'Eternal Son'. They describe the risen Lord Jesus as 'ever living', but not living from eternity except in the mind of God. They testify to the risen Lord Jesus at the right hand of God, serving as a high priest to intercede for believers. For instance consider Hebrews:

But this man, because he continueth ever, hath an unchangeable priesthood.

Wherefore he is able also to save them to the uttermost that come unto God by him, seeing he ever liveth to make intercession for them ...

We have such an high priest, who is set on the right hand of the throne of the Majesty of the heavens

(Hebrews 7:24 - 8:1)

No 'God the Son' could mediate between God and man. Only the man Christ Jesus, who shed his blood for us, could do such a thing.

Texts suggesting the Holy Spirit is a distinct person

The main evidence for 'God the Spirit' comes from John chapters 14-16. Some of the main texts are John 14:16-18, 23, 15:26, 16:13f.

Chapter 6 examines these texts and the general trinitarian argument. The main reason the argument fails is that the use of personal pronouns in Greek does not indicate a person.

Conclusions

A trinitarian would claim to find a Trinity in the Old Testament. Certainly the Old Testament contains descriptions of God acting in different personal ways, and different terms such as 'Word', Wisdom' and 'Spirit' are used for this. However this does not amount to proof that God is a Trinity of three independently existing 'Persons'.

Biblical evidence for a Trinity

- **Old Testament evidence for the plurality of God is weak**
- **'trinitarian' texts in the New Testament do not show three 'Persons' but show God acting through Christ and the Spirit**
- **The New Testament texts cited for the three individual 'Persons' do not prove a Trinity**

In the next three chapters the biblical evidence for the three 'Persons' of the Trinity will be examined more closely.

4. THE MYTH OF 'GOD THE FATHER'

The 'First Person' of the Trinity cannot be found in the Bible

References to 'the Father' and to 'God the Father' are in fact to God Himself, not to a 'First Person' of a Trinity

Who is the 'God the Father'?

A trinitarian speaks about 'God the Father', 'God the Son' and 'God the Spirit', and assumes that these titles refer to different persons within the Godhead.

But who is 'God the Father'? Is he the 'First Person' of three Persons of a Trinity, or is He God Himself? In this chapter we will examine the biblical evidence, and conclude that a 'First Person' is nowhere to be found in scripture.

'God the Father' is indeed a biblical term (unlike the titles 'God the Son' and 'God the Spirit'). Therefore a trinitarian might think it reasonable that the title 'God the Father' when used in the Bible refers to the 'First Person' of the Trinity. However this is not the case. When we look at the biblical contexts we find that all the titles that a trinitarian might suppose to refer to a First Person actually refer to God himself, and not to a 'First Person'.

First of all consider again the arguments made in Chapter 3. 'trinitarian texts' that are cited to prove a Trinity mention three persons or three personal aspects of God. The second member of the trio is normally Jesus Christ, or 'the Son'. The third member is the Spirit. But who is the first member?

The first member of such a trio is never a 'First Person' of the Trinity, but *in every case is God Himself.* Many times this is made absolutely clear by the use of the word 'God', rather than 'the Father' or 'God the Father' as a trinitarian might prefer. To illustrate this, consider two important 'trinitarian' verses:

Come ye near unto me, hear ye this; I have not spoken in secret from the beginning; from the time that it was, there am I: and now the Lord God, and his Spirit, hath sent me (Isaiah 48:16)

And the grace of the Lord Jesus Christ, and the love of God, and the communion of the Holy Ghost, be with you all (2 Corinthians 13:14)

Isaiah 48:16 is taken to be an instance of the three Persons of the Trinity distinguished from each other. According to the Trinity the person speaking is 'God the Son', or the pre-existent Word (Logos) of God. But the speaker is sent by the Lord God (*Yahweh Elohim*), not a 'God the Father'. There is no 'God the Father' here.

The trinitarian reading of 2 Corinthians 13:14 sees three divine Persons. But the verse mentions the love of *God*, not 'the love of God the Father' or 'the love of the First Person'. 'God' refers to God in his entirety, not to a 'First Person'. There is no 'First Person' in this verse. Paul talks about the Lord Jesus Christ, not a pre-existent Son of God. The verse is describing three aspects of God's activity, but does not show God as a Trinity.

So, if 'trinitarian' texts do not seem to show a 'First Person', where can the 'God the Father' be found in the Bible? First consider the problem of identifying the voice of 'God the Father'.

The voice of 'God the Father' is that of God

When God speaks, does he sometimes speak as the voice of all three 'Persons', or does He sometimes speak as 'God the Father' only? A trinitarian would have to say that when God is reported as speaking as *God* in His entirety, he speaks as the whole Trinity together, but there must be some occasions when the voice is that of either the 'God the Father' or 'God the Son' or 'God the Spirit' speaking singly. This would have to be so, otherwise it would be nonsense to say that God is three Persons. Each 'Person' of the Trinity must at least have his own voice, otherwise he could not be a different 'person' from the other two.

So is it possible to go through the Bible looking at the texts where God is recorded as speaking and identifying which texts record the whole Trinity speaking in unison, and which ones record just 'God the Father' speaking? If God really is three different Persons, then it should be a straightforward task to identify the speaker in every case. In the John Ankerberg debate, the trinitarian representatives did make this claim[94].

---

94 J. Ankerberg at al, 1985.

For instance, a trinitarian would have to say that the voice from heaven at Jesus' baptism is that of the 'First Person' of the Trinity, not of the whole Trinity speaking, because the voice speaks about the so-called 'Second Person' as somebody different.

Then, after the Ascension, when God speaks it is presumably with the voice of the whole Trinity. For instance, when God speaks to Peter in Acts 10:15 'What God hath cleansed, that call not thou common', the trinitarian would say that God speaks here as a Trinity.

However these attempts to distinguish between the voices of the 'Persons' run into difficulty. How can the voices in the Old Testament be distinguished? In Chapter 3 it was noted that God talks of himself as 'I' thousands of times, compared with only a handful where he uses 'we' or 'us'. For instance:

I am the Lord that maketh all things; that stretcheth forth the heavens alone; that spreadeth abroad the earth by myself (Isaiah 44:24)

According to the Trinity, each time in out of thousands of cases that God talks of himself as 'I', or 'I alone', he is speaking as three persons talking together, as a kind of 'singular trio'. How could the Bible be this obscure? Jews read their sacred scriptures and understand 'I' when God speaks as meaning singularity. Trinitarians seem to put themselves in the position of telling a Jew that the 'I' in their scriptures is really as a kind of disguised 'we'.

In fact, in all the cases which trinitarian argument might propose as those where the voice of the 'God the Father' can be heard, we find on closer examination that it is *God* speaking, not a 'God the Father'. For instance the voice at the baptism of Jesus was shown (in Chapter 3) to be God speaking, not a 'First Person'. We cannot find an instance anywhere in the Bible of the voice of a 'God the Father' distinguishable from God himself.

'Father' in the New Testament means 'God'

Trinitarian teaching is sometimes unclear about whether the terms 'the Father' (used of God) and 'God' have different references. According to the classical Trinity, the term 'the Father' should refer only to the 'First Person', but 'God' refers to the whole triune God, all three 'Persons' together. However there is a fundamental problem for the Trinity on this point, because biblical usage does not distinguish between 'the Father' and 'God'. 'The Father' is used as another term for 'God'.

Most trinitarians would tend to recognise this last point, and this leads to some confusion in trinitarian use of the term 'the Father'. When a trinitarian speaks of 'the Father' he may mean 'God' (in his supposed triunity) and sometimes 'the First Person' of the Trinity. The confusion is understandable, but it comes from the doctrine of the Trinity, not from the Bible.

Jesus was the first to refer to God as 'Father' in the personal sense. In the Old Testament God is referred to as 'Father' only eight times but not in a personal sense[xlii]. He was Father only in the creative sense, as father of the nation Israel. Christians believe that it is only because Jesus was able to call God 'Father' that believers are able to do likewise. Jesus taught his disciples to pray 'Our Father...'. This was a new understanding of God.

Jesus while on earth refers to God as 'God', 'my God', 'your God', 'my Father', 'O Father', 'Father', 'the Father', 'your Father' (to his disciples) with no distinction in reference between the terms. They are all terms referring to God. For instance compare

... pray to thy Father in secret ... (Matthew 6:6)

I thank thee, O Father, Lord of heaven and earth, ... even so, Father: for so it seemed good in thy sight. All things are delivered unto me of my Father: and no man knoweth the Son, but the Father ... (Matthew 11:25ff/Luke 10:21f)

For the Son of Man shall come in the glory of his Father with his angels ... (Matthew 16:27)

But of that day and hour knoweth no man, ... but my Father only (Matthew 26:36)

I ... came forth from God ... he sent me' (John 8:42)

I came forth from the Father ... (John 16:28)

O Father, glorify thou me ... with the glory which I had with thee before the world was (John 17:5)

I ascend unto my Father, and your Father: and to my God, and your God (John 20:17)[xliii]

In these passages 'Father' and 'God' clearly refer to the same person. There is no trinitarian usage of 'Father' as a 'First Person' who could be distinguishable from God as a whole. In the last quote from John 20, Jesus is not referring to two (or four) different persons, or even two different aspects or roles of the same persons.

The same usage of 'Father' to refer to 'God' is used in the rest of the New Testament. God can be referred to as 'Father' because now, by virtue of Jesus Christ having died and ascended to heaven, He is the Father of all believers. Christians are children of God because of adoption, because they have received the Spirit of Christ, as Paul makes clear:

...ye have received the Spirit of adoption, whereby we cry Abba, Father.

The Spirit itself beareth witness with our spirit, that we are the children of God (Romans 8:15f cf Galatians 4:6).

'The Father' is used to refer to God in numerous places throughout the epistles, for instance Romans 6:4, Ephesians 2:18, 3:14, Colossians 1:12, 19, 1 Peter 1:17, 1 John 1:2, 3, 2:1, 13, 15, 16, 22, 23, 24, 3:1, 4:14. In all of these cases, the words 'the Father' could be replaced by 'God' and the text would have the same meaning. Nowhere in the New Testament is there a 'Father' who is just one Person of a Trinity.

In many texts, such as the greetings at the beginning of epistles, God is referred to as 'God the Father', 'God our Father', 'God and Father', 'God and the Father of our Lord Jesus Christ', 'God, even the Father of our Lord Jesus Christ' or 'God and our Father'. Some trinitarians would say that these terms identify the 'First Person' of the Trinity. However these terms also are just different ways of referring to God.

'God our Father' means 'God'

'God our Father' (KJV translation) is used ten times in the salutations in Paul's epistles (Romans 1:7, 1 Corinthians 1:3, 2 Corinthians 1:2, Ephesians 1:2, Philippians 1:2, Colossians 1:2, 1 Thessalonians 1:1, 2 Thessalonians 1:2, 1 Timothy 1:2, Philemon 1:3). For instance

Grace to you and peace from God our Father and from the Lord Jesus Christ (Romans 1:7)

In these passages there is no word for 'and' (the Greek *kai*) in between 'God' and 'our Father'. In the contexts it is always clear that 'our Father' is used as a description for God.

'God and Father' means 'God'

The phrases 'God and Father', and similar phrases like 'God and the Father'. 'God and his (Jesus') Father' and 'God and our Father', 'God even the Father' occur several times in the New Testament, mostly in the epistles. On all occasions it is clear that God himself is being referred to, and 'Father' does not indicate a separate person from God. Rather, 'Father' is used as a way of describing who God is. 'God and Father' is a term for God, telling the reader that this is the God who is the Father of Jesus Christ and the Father of believers.

All the original Greek texts except Colossians 1:3, Colossians 3:17[95] and 2 Thessalonians 2:16 have the Greek word *kai* between 'God' and 'Father'. This word can be translated as 'and' indicating two different objects. However but it can also be used to indicate two different descriptions for the *same* thing. In some cases the KJV translates *kai* as 'even', indicating this understanding. In none of the texts is there a definite article 'the' in front of 'Father', which indicates again that the two things referred to are indeed the same.

The KJV translates *kai* as 'and' in twelve cases:

The God and Father of our Lord Jesus Christ, he who is blessed for ever, knows that I do not lie. (2 Corinthians 11:31)

Who gave himself for our sins, that he might deliver us from this present evil world, according to the will of God and our Father (Galatians 1:4)

Blessed be the God and Father of our Lord Jesus Christ, who has blessed us in Christ with every spiritual blessing in the heavenly places (Ephesians 1:3)

... one God and Father of us all, who is above all and through all in all (Ephesians 4:6)

Giving thanks always for all things unto God and the Father ... (Ephesians 5:20)

Now unto God and our Father be glory for ever and ever (Philippians 4:20)

We give thanks to God and the Father of our Lord Jesus Christ ... (Colossians 1:3)

And whatsoever ye do in word or deed, do all in the name of the Lord Jesus, giving thanks to God and the Father by him (Colossians 3:17)

Remembering without ceasing your work of faith, and labour of love, and patience of hope in our Lord Jesus Christ, in the sight of God and our Father (1 Thessalonians 1:3)

[95] Other translations (e.g. RSV and NIV) translate Colossians 1:3 and Colossians 3:17 more correctly as 'God the Father' rather than 'God and the Father'. See the following section 'God the Father'.

Now God himself and our Father, and our Lord Jesus Christ direct our way unto you (1 Thessalonians 3:11)

Blessed be the God and Father of our Lord Jesus Christ (1 Peter 1:3)

And hath made us kings and priests unto God and his Father (Revelation 1:6)

The KJV translates *kai* as 'even' in the following six texts (which the NIV and RSV render as 'God and Father', 'God the Father' or 'God our Father'):

That ye may ... glorify God, even the Father of our Lord Jesus Christ (Romans 15:6)

Then cometh the end, when he shall have delivered up the kingdom to God, even the Father ... (1 Corinthian 15:24)

Blessed be God, even the Father of our Lord Jesus Christ ... (2 Corinthians 1:3)

To the end he may stablish your hearts unblameable in holiness before God, even our Father ... (1 Thessalonians 3:13)

Now our Lord Jesus Christ himself, and God, even our Father, which hath loved us ... (2 Thessalonians 2:16)

Therewith bless we God, even the Father ... (James 3:9)[xliv]

In all of these texts, God is being referred to. A trinitarian would probably agree that 'God' and 'the Father' refer to the same person or being, and the KJV translations of *kai* as 'even' in the last six texts make this clear.

Furthermore the use of 'Father' is to describe God in his relationships. It is God himself who is the Father of Jesus Christ and the Father of believers. Therefore God can be described as 'God and Father ...'.

In all these passages, as with the words of Jesus, there is no trinitarian use of 'Father'. God is described as 'our Father', 'the Father', 'the Father of Jesus Christ', 'God and Father', 'God our Father' in ways and contexts that make it clear that these are all different ways of referring to God. The New Testament makes no distinction between a triune God who is all three 'Persons' and a 'Father' who is just one of those 'Persons'.

'God the Father' means 'God'

The term 'God the Father' has a special place in the doctrine of the Trinity, as it is believed to be the correct designation for the so-called 'First Person'. However biblical usage does not support this.

'God the Father' does indeed occur in the Bible, unlike 'God the Son' and 'God the Spirit' which appear nowhere in scripture. 'God the Father' occurs thirteen times in the King James translation of the New Testament, and the NIV and RSC add a few more to these, e.g. Colossians 1:3 and 3:17 which the KJV renders 'God and the Father'.

In most cases the original Greek text consists of the words for 'God' and 'Father' next to each other without a definite article 'the' in front of either. For example, in Galatians 1:3 'from God the Father' translates *απο θεου πατροσ*, and in 1 Thessalonians 1:1 'in God the Father' translates *εν θεω πατρι*. There are only two exceptions to this, John 6:27 and 1 Corinthians 8:6, which we shall discuss separately.

'God the Father' is used in similar contexts to the other terms like 'God our Father' and 'God and Father' and with the same meaning. 'God the Father' refers to God Himself and not a 'First Person' of a Trinity. Many of these contexts are the greetings and blessings in the epistles. The greeting is from God and from the risen Jesus. A trinitarian may deny this, and say that the greetings are from the 'First Person' and the 'Second Person' of the Trinity. However the contexts make it clear that the 'God the Father' refers to God and not 'First Person'.

First consider the greetings. **'God the Father'** is shown in bold to aid comparison:

Grace to you and peace from God our Father and from the Lord Jesus Christ (Romans 1:7)

Grace be unto you, and peace, from God our Father and from the Lord Jesus Christ (1 Corinthians 1:3)

Blessed be God, even the Father of our Lord Jesus Christ ... (2 Corinthians 1:3)

Grace be to you and peace from **God the Father** *and from the Lord Jesus Christ ... according to the will of God our Father (Galatians 1:3f)*

Grace be to you, and peace, from God our Father and from the Lord Jesus Christ Blessed be the God and Father of our Lord Jesus Christ ... (Ephesians 1:2f)

Peace be to the brethren ... from **God the Father** *and the Lord Jesus Christ (Ephesians 6:23)*

Grace be unto you, and peace, from God our Father and from the Lord Jesus Christ (Philippians 1:2)

Grace be unto you, and peace, from God our Father and from the Lord Jesus Christ. We give thanks to God and the Father (NIV and RSV **God the Father***) of our Lord Jesus Christ ... (Colossians 1:2f)*

Grace be unto you, and peace, from God our Father and from the Lord Jesus Christ (1 Thessalonians 1:1)

Grace unto you, and peace, from God our Father and from the Lord Jesus Christ (2 Thessalonians 1:2)

Grace, mercy and peace, from God our Father and from the Lord Jesus Christ (1 Timothy 1:2)

Grace, mercy and peace, from **God the Father** *and Christ Jesus our Lord (2 Timothy 1:2)*

Grace, mercy and peace, from **God the Father** *and the Lord Jesus Christ our Saviour (Titus 1:4)*

Grace to you, and peace, from God our Father and from the Lord Jesus Christ (Philemon 3)

Elect according to the foreknowledge of **God the Father**, ... *Blessed be the God and Father of our Lord Jesus Christ ... (1 Peter 1:2f)*

Grace be with you, mercy and peace, from **God the Father** *and from the Lord Jesus Christ (2 John 3)*

Jude, the servant of Jesus Christ ... to them that are sanctified by **God the Father** *... (Jude 1)*

In all but four of his greetings Paul uses 'God our Father', but in Galatians, Ephesians (at the end but not the beginning), 2 Timothy and Titus he uses 'God the Father' (in bold). The contexts for the greetings are the same. 'God our Father' clearly refers to God himself, in his entirety (see above) and not a First Person distinguished from a Second Person. There is nothing to indicate that Paul is using 'God the Father' in any way but to refer to God in his entirety.

The use of 'God the Father' in Peter's greeting next to 'God and Father of our Lord Jesus Christ' indicates that the writer is also using 'God the Father' to refer to God. The same might be inferred from the contexts in 2 John and Jude.

Here are the other instances of 'God the Father':

Labour not for the meat that perisheth, but for that meat which endureth unto everlasting life, which the Son of man shall give unto you: for him hath **God the Father** *sealed (John 6:27)*

But to us there is but one **God, the Father**, *of whom are all things ... and one Lord Jesus Christ by whom are all things, and we by him. (1 Corinthians 8:6 cf Ephesians 4:4-6)*

One God and Father of all, who is above all, and through all, and in you all (Ephesians 4:4-6)

Paul, an apostle ... but by Jesus Christ, and **God the Father**, *who raised him from the dead .. (Galatians 1:1)*

And every tongue shall confess that Jesus Christ is Lord, to the glory of **God the Father** *(Philippians 2:11)*

And whatsoever ye do in word or deed, do all in the name of the Lord Jesus, giving thanks to God and the Father (NIV and RSV **God the Father***) by him (Colossians 3:17)*

For he received from **God the Father** *honour and glory ... (2 Peter 1:17)*

In the Greek text of John 6:27 the words for 'God' and 'Father' both have 'the' in front of them with the word for 'sealed' in between them, so that the passage reads 'for this one the Father sealed (the) God'. The Greek text is therefore quite different from anything considered before. 'God the Father' is a natural translation, but it would be a bold step to claim that it must refer to a 'First Person'. We should remember that Jesus often talked of God as 'the Father', and so it would be natural to presume he is doing the same here.

The texts from Galatians, Philippians and Colossians are close to where Paul evidently uses 'God the Father' to refer to God in the greetings (see above), and there is no indication that Paul here, or anywhere else, is using the words 'God' and 'Father' together in any way but to refer to God himself.

In 1 Corinthians 8:6, unlike all the texts above, the word for 'Father' has the definite article 'the' before it, so that it reads in the Greek the same as it does in the translations. Does this indicate the trinitarian 'First Person'? The first point to make here is that the translators of the KJV, RSV and NIV all insert a comma between 'God' and 'the Father', showing that they believe that 'the Father' is just a qualifying description of God (just like all the other texts examined above). So if 1 Corinthians 8:6 speaks of a 'First Person', this trinitarian belief is not shared by the major English translations.

Secondly, the statement in 1 Corinthians 8:6 that there is only one God (the Father) surely applies to God himself not a 'First Person'. The context of the passage is to emphasize monotheism in the face of worship of the other supposed 'gods' to whom meat is being offered (and which some Corinthians are eating to the offence of their brothers). Paul's purpose here would not be to emphasize the doctrine of the Trinity, even if he believed in it.

Thirdly, if this verse did teach a 'First Person' of the Trinity, and the above analysis is accepted, 1 Corinthians 8:6 would be the only place in his letters where Paul does teach a Trinity. If Paul did believe in a Trinity, a doctrine of that importance would surely have taken a central place in, say, the Letter to the Romans, not referred to only in a section of 1 Corinthians dealing with food offered to idols.

We can therefore conclude that in the texts of which are translated 'God the Father', there is no implication of a reference to a 'First Person' in a Trinity. 'God the Father', like the other references such as 'God our Father', 'God and the Father of our Lord Jesus Christ', refers to God himself. There is no trinitarian 'God the Father' in the New Testament.

Trinitarian reply: 'God' refers to 'God the Father'

A trinitarian might try to turn these criticisms on their head by saying that the terms 'God', 'God our Father', 'the Father' etc. are actually used in scripture to refer to the First Person of the Trinity.

Gregory Boyd, in *Oneness Pentecostals and the Trinity*, makes this argument. He argues that in the 'Trinitarian verses' (see Chapter 3) where God (or 'the Father'), Christ (or 'the Son') and the Spirit are all spoken of together, it is the three Persons of the Trinity that are being talked about, as against the Oneness Pentecostal view that only 'the Father' is divine. Boyd interprets oneness pentecostals as saying that 'the Father' refers to the divine aspect of Jesus and 'the Son' the human aspect.

Boyd argues (quite correctly) that oneness pentecostals would not deny that the Spirit is divine and he also says that the title 'Lord' applied to Jesus indicates divinity. The first point is correct, but the second is debatable[xlv]. But even if Boyd is correct and 'Father', 'Son' and 'Spirit' all refer to aspects of God, this does not prove that the three Persons of the Trinity are being referred to. Why does 'God' not refer to God Himself, rather than a First Person? Boyd continues:

> Hence the attempt to restrict divinity to the Father, when he and the Son (and the Spirit) are being distinguished, simply fails. A much better explanation for why the Father is usually alone called God when spoken of in the same context as the Son and the Spirit ... is simply that it was

> customary, as a matter of literary convention, for the New Testament authors to do so.[96]

Boyd includes an endnote to explain further why 'the Father' is alone called God:

> In traditional trinitarian terminology the Father is perceived of as being 'the beginning and source' of the Trinity, not in a temporal sense, but in an ontological sense.[97]

Boyd assumes in the first place that there is a 'First Person', and then further assumes that it was literary convention to call this 'First Person' by the title of 'God'. Boyd does not give any evidence for either assumption.

Boyd's endnote indicates the reliance of trinitarian argument upon 'traditional terminology' in saying that 'God the Father' is 'the beginning and source of the Trinity'. The fact that something is traditionally believed does not make it true. If the 'God the Father' is 'the beginning and source of the Trinity' then the First Person comes first and the other two come second and third and take their being from the First Person[xlvi]. Such a First Person cannot be the First Person of the classical Trinity, because all the 'Persons' of the classical Trinity are supposedly co-equal and co-eternal[xlvii].

Boyd continues his argument:

> We find in the Old Testament ... the development of a way of speaking about God that preserved God's transcendence while also emphasizing the reality of his involvement with the world. Authors frequently distinguished 'God' from 'his Spirit', 'his wisdom', 'his hand', 'his Word' etc .... to 'provide expressions of God's immanence without compromising his transcendence' (quote from Dunn, *Christology in the Making*). To speak of any of God's attributes as distinct from himself was simply to speak of God himself involved in the world ... None of this changes when we get to the New Testament, except that here we have a clear revelation that God's 'Word' and God's 'Spirit' are terms that can be used to refer to two personally distinct ways in which God is God, and not simply different forms of God's activity ... Thus, for New Testament authors to refer to 'God' (or 'Father'), 'Jesus' (or 'Son') and 'the Holy Spirit' together in the same context ... is simply for them to refer to the totality of God in his threefold way of existing. It is a

---

[96] Boyd, *Oneness Pentecostals and the Trinity*, p57.

[97] Boyd, *Oneness Pentecostals and the Trinity*, p230.

way of saying 'God/God/God', but in a much richer and more felicitous manner.[98]

This is an example of a trinitarian argument that replaces 'two attributes' with 'three persons' and moves from a 'weak' understanding of 'person' to a 'strong' sense (see Chapter 1). Boyd describes how in the Old Testament 'God' could be spoken of alongside His attributes, Word and Spirit, without implying that the Word and the Spirit were not God also. He said that the same applies in the New Testament except for the 'clear revelation' that there are now 'two personally distinct ways in which God is God'.

Boyd moves from two attributes of God, Word and Spirit, to God's 'threefold way of existing'. *Attributes* have become *personally distinct ways of existing* and *two* has become *three*. The only justification stated here is that of 'clear revelation'.

In his arguments Boyd assumes the existence of a 'God the Father' in his attempt to prove it. He assumes that there was a literary convention to refer to the 'God the Father' as God'. He assumes that there is a clear revelation that the Son and the Spirit are two 'persons' in the Godhead. He assumes that God has a threefold way of existing. None of these assumptions can be justified from the Bible. It is an example of how trinitarian argument sometimes assumes what it needs to prove.

The truth in Boyd's arguments lies in the fact that the Son and their Spirit *do* take their being from 'the Father'. However 'the Father' is not a trinitarian First Person but is God himself who is the author of all. The classical Trinity cannot be reconciled with the biblical fact that 'the Father' is not the equal of the Son and the Spirit but is their superior and their author.

Those who would try to maintain that there is a trinitarian 'First Person' would cite biblical acts that can be attributed just to a 'God the Father'. For instance the act of creation is said to be an act 'appropriate' to 'the Father' (see Chapter 2). But there is no 'Father' other than God in the Bible. Creation was an act of *God* as a whole and cannot be labelled as particularly the responsibility of some 'First Person'. Some may cite particular miraculous acts, such as the parting of the Red Sea and the resurrection of Jesus as the responsibility of 'the Father'. However the objection is the same. 'The Father' is the same as God. It was

---

[98] Boyd, *Oneness Pentecostals and the Trinity*, pp57-58.

God who parted the Red Sea. It was *God* who raised Jesus from the dead[99]. The Bible does not tell us about a 'Father' who is different from God.

Conclusions

The New Testament use of 'the Father' has the same reference as 'God'. The trinitarian 'God the Father' has no scriptural foundation.

'The Father' and 'God the Father' in the New Testament

- **Jesus used 'the Father', 'my Father', 'your Father' as terms for God, not a First Person**
- **'The Father' and similar terms refer to God, not a First Person**
- **There is no trinitarian sense of 'God the Father' in the New Testament**

The next two chapters shall examine the doctrines of the 'God the Son' and the 'God the Spirit' and show that there is no biblical foundation to these doctrines either. There are no Second and Third Persons, co-equal and co-eternal with some 'First Person'.

[99] Acts 2:32, Romans 8:11 with Romans 8:9 showing that 'God' is the one who raised Jesus.

5. THE ERROR OF THE 'ETERNAL SON'

A 'Second Person' of a Trinity cannot be found in the Bible

An 'Eternal Son' violates the humanity of Jesus

An 'Eternal Son' cannot be begotten

Texts for an 'Eternal Son' can be seen in terms of the begotten Son

Trinitarian explanations using 'two natures' are unsuccessful

The doctrine of the 'Eternal Son'

According to the classical Trinity Jesus Christ was the incarnation of the Second Person, the 'Eternal Son'. A trinitarian finds evidence for this doctrine mainly in John's Gospel, Philippians, Colossians and 1 John[100]. Trinitarians believe that Jesus thought and spoke as someone who

a) existed before he was born

b) was an agent of creation on behalf of 'God the Father'

c) was sent to earth by 'God the Father'

d) will return to 'God the Father'

A trinitarian would understand that the Prologue to John's Gospel is talking about Jesus Christ when it says 'In the beginning was the Word'. He believes that, when Jesus talks, he talks with memory, will and emotions of the Eternal Son. He has the *identity* and the *personality* of the Second Person of the Trinity. For instance when Jesus said:

"I came down from heaven, not to do mine own will, but the will of him who sent me"

(John 6:38)

the trinitarian interpretation is that Jesus was talking about his memory of his descent from heaven, and about the will of the Second Person which was subordinate to the will of the First Person. When Jesus said:

---

100 The main texts supporting an 'Eternal Son' doctrine are John 1:1-14, 6:38, 44, 51, 62, 7:29, 8:23, 42, 58, 9:5, 39, 14:2, 28, 17:5, 24, 1 Corinthians 8:6, Galatians 4:4, Ephesians 3:9, Philippians 2:6-9, Colossians 1:15-19, Hebrews 1:1-10 and 1 John 1:1f.

"Glorify thou me ... with the glory which I had with thee before the world was" (John 17:5) the trinitarian understanding is that Jesus is talking with the memory of the Eternal Son who was there in the beginning with the Father.

The trinitarian would say that it is a *strength* of the Trinity that it can account for passages like these in terms of the eternal 'God the Son' talking. Indeed many trinitarians would say that it is *only* because of the need to account for passages like these that they believe in a Trinity[101].

The problem for the doctrine of the 'Eternal Son' is that this interpretation of such sayings of Christ contradicts the authentic humanity of Jesus. In this chapter it is argued that Jesus thought and spoke as a man *at all times*. At no time did he think and speak with the identity of an 'Eternal Son'. Then we will show how the doctrine of the 'Eternal Son' contradicts scripture, and why the texts that are used to support the doctrine should be given alternative interpretations. Finally two well-known trinitarian arguments are discussed.

Did Jesus have a split personality?

Christians acknowledge that Jesus was the perfect man. Not only was Christ the perfect man, he was an *authentic* and *individual* human being whilst also being the Word of God made flesh (John 1:14). But this leaves unanswered some obvious quesrions. How could Jesus be both man and God? As a man, was Jesus *aware* that he was God or the Second Person of a Trinity? Did he have one will or two? Did he have one set of memories as a man, and another set of memories reaching back to his 'time with the Father' before Creation? Did he have a split personality or an integrated personality? These issues have been debated for seventeen hundred years.

The trinitarian scholar Gregory Boyd attacks oneness pentecostalism for splitting Christ into two[102]. However the doctrine of the Trinity is open to the same charge.

There are two alternative beliefs about the earthly life of Jesus:

Either

---

[101] E. Calvin Beisner expressed this belief on the John Ankerberg Show (J. Ankerberg , 1985).

[102] G. Boyd, *Oneness Pentecostals and the Trinity*, p58. Quoted at more length below.

Jesus thought and spoke at *some* times as a man and at *other* times as God or a pre-existent 'Son'.

or

Jesus thought and spoke like a man at *all* times.

The alternatives are genuine and clear. One or the other must be true.

The classical trinitarian view of the earthly life of Jesus can be simply stated. Jesus was *one person* with two natures, divine and human, a so-called 'God-man'. He was God by virtue of being the incarnation of the Second Person of the Trinity. Therefore he could think and speak both as a man and as 'God the Son'. At some times Jesus could pray to God by virtue of his human nature and at other times he can speak with the personality of 'God the Son' (such as in John 6:38 and 17:5, quoted above) by virtue of his divine nature. On this view Jesus must be operating with some kind of divine self-consciousness when he performed miracles, and that with some kind of divine omniscience when he read people's thoughts. This divine self-awareness is supposed to sit alongside his human self-awareness, and his divine omniscience to somehow co-exist with human ignorance. Jesus had a human will which at times is contrasted with the will of the Father (Matthew 26:39. John 6:38); for the trinitarian this implies two wills in Christ, the human will and the divine will[103].

The 'God-man' 'two natures' views of Jesus implies that at times Jesus speaks and thinks out of his divine nature when he performs miracles, reads thoughts or forgives sins. At other times he speaks and thinks about his human nature when he shows human weakness, human ignorance or submits his will to the Father's will. The trinitarian position requires Jesus to have the personality and memory of an authentic human being *alongside* the personality and memory of an 'Eternal Son' who can remember his time with 'the Father'. According to this view Jesus could have spoken like this:

"I am a man, but I am also 'God the Son' in disguise. Most of the times I am not aware of my deity and behave just as a normal human being. But sometimes I become aware of my true being, and talk about my time with the Father before the creation of the world."

In other words, a believer in the classical Trinity has to believe that Jesus had some kind of split personality, with two sets of memories, two sets of

---

[103] The Council of Constantinople in 680 declared that there are two wills in Christ, but only one person. See Chapter 2.

knowledge and two wills. According to the Trinity, Jesus could think and speak *sometimes* as man and *sometimes* as 'God the Son'.

This understanding must surely be incorrect. How could Jesus have an *integrated* and *truly human* personality if he had both a divine and a human self-awareness, switching between them as the occasion demanded? How could a person with an integrated personality be sometimes omniscient, and sometimes ignorant of things (for instance the time of his coming, Mark 13:32)? When Jesus talked about being sent down from heaven (John 6:38) or about the glory he had with the Father before the world was (John 17:5), *who* was talking? Was this the single personality who was both the man born in Bethlehem and the 'Eternal Son'? It cannot surely be both.

It is possible to be trinitarian without believing that Jesus had a divine awareness that he was 'God the Son'. The Anglican Bishop of Durham, Tom Wright, in *Jesus and the Identity of God*, asks the question 'In what sense might Jesus conceivably have thought about himself as God?' He defends the conservative view that Jesus did think of himself as 'God' in the sense of fulfilling first century Jewish ideas of how God would return to and redeem his people. For instance Wright says that Jesus could well have thought of himself as dying for their sins. However Wright maintains that our view of Jesus must do full justice to his humanity:

> … I cannot think that an orthodox Christology, which takes Jesus' humanity at least as seriously as Chalcedon did, can avoid asking how Jesus could think thoughts like that (of himself as the embodiment of Israel's God) precisely as a second-Temple Jew. Unless we are prepared to address the question in those terms we are simply being Apollinarian, producing a Jesus with a human body but a divine mind. And the New Testament own christolology forbids me to suppose that such a hybrid does justice to God, to Jesus, or to salvation.

Wright concludes:

> I do not think Jesus 'knew he was God' in the same sense that one knows one is tired or happy, male of female. He did not sit back and say to himself "Well. I never! I'm the second person of the Trinity!" Rather, as part of his human vocation grasped in faith, sustained in prayer, tested in confrontation, agonized over in further prayer and doubt, and implemented in action, he believed he had to do and to be … that which according to scripture only YHWH himself could do and be.[104]

---

104 N.T. Wright, *Jesus and the Identity of God*, pp12, 16.

Jesus is a complete, authentic, human being, 'in all things made like unto his brethren' (Hebrews 2:17), 'in all points tempted as we are, yet without sin' (Hebrews 4:15). No authentic and sane human being could have memories of a pre-existent life as a 'God the Son'. The biblical picture of Jesus cannot be that of a man who sometimes appears to remember a past life and at other times to forget it. To say that Jesus was a 'God-man' does not provide an explanation for this.

The truth is that Jesus was a man subject to all the constraints and rules that all humans are subject to. *At all times* in his life, he had to regard God as other than himself, pray to God, and give all glory to God. Jesus is the perfect man giving all glory to the Father. Whenever Jesus talks about 'the Father', he is referring to *God* and not a 'First Person' (see Chapter 4). Jesus talked about 'the Father' as greater than himself (John 14:28), he prayed to the Father and called the Father 'my God'. Only a man could do those things. Prayer happens between man and God, *never* between two divine personages. A co-equal 'God the Son' could not correctly regard the 'God the Father' as equal to himself.

Just because Jesus performed miracles, it does not follow that he did so with a divine self-consciousness. He always claimed that he did so with the power that God had given him, and he always acknowledged God as the source. He said the he could do nothing of himself, but only what he saw the Father doing (John 5:19). On his resurrection he said that all authority had been *given* to him (Matthew 28:18). He could forgive sins because the authority had been given to him by God. He never claimed to exercise power as God himself. Jesus must be talking and thinking *as a man* when he talks about God, when he prays, when he heals people, when he performs miracles.

Never during his life does Jesus think or talk with the consciousness of a 'God the Son', because to do so would make him the 'hybrid' that Bishop Wright refers to, and other than a complete, authentic and sane man. Jesus is always talking and thinking as a man, even when he is aware of his unique relationship to God and of his calling to die for the sins of his people[xlviii].

No 'First Person' implies no 'Second Person'

In the preceding chapter it was pointed out that there is no 'God the Father' in the Bible. If there is no First Person of a Trinity then there can be no Second or Third Persons either.

There is no 'God the Son' in the Bible

According to the Trinity, Jesus Christ is the incarnation of a 'God the Son', a pre-existent divine being who descends from heaven and voluntarily gives up his powers. Trinitarian argument interprets Philippians 2:5-11 in this way.[105] However the term 'God the Son' does not occur in the Bible. No New Testament writer uses the phrase 'God the Son' or 'Eternal Son'.

In fact the biblical context for the term 'Son' properly refers to a *man*, not to a divine person. In the Bible, the term 'Son of God' is never used to apply to a unique pre-existent 'Second Person'. In the Old Testament, it has three types of reference[106]: (i) angels or heavenly beings (e.g. Ps 82:6), (ii) the nation of Israel (e.g. Hosea 11:1) (iii) the king of Israel (e.g. Ps 2:7[xlix]). In the New Testament, the term 'Son' when used of Jesus refers to the Son of God, *the man Jesus Christ* who was born in Bethlehem, not to a pre-existent 'Eternal Son'[l].

The gospels do not show the interaction of two divine personages, a 'God the Father' in heaven and a 'God the Son' on earth. The gospels show the relationship between *God* on the one hand, and the perfect man Jesus on the other hand. Not only did Jesus say that the Father was greater than he (John 14:28), but he said that he of himself *could do nothing but only as the Father willed or taught* (John 5:30, 8:28),. He sought not his own will but the will of the Father (John 5:30, 6:38). Jesus was, and is, a perfect man living in obedience to God, not a 'God the Son'. There is no 'God the Son' in the Bible.

An 'Eternal Son' is a theological error

When and how did the doctrine of the 'God the Son' come about? Chapter 2 described its development from the 'Logos doctrine' of the second century Apologists. According to what Lampe called a 'double projection', the personality of Jesus was projected onto the Logos, the Logos was called 'the Son' and considered to have a human personality. The personality of this supposed Eternal Son was then projected back into the earthly life of Jesus, to interpret sayings of Jesus such as "I came down from heaven ..." (John 6:38) or " ... the glory which I had with thee before the world was " (John 17:5) in terms of a life that the Eternal Son was supposed to have lived before the Incarnation.

---

105 See below for an alternative interpretation of Philippians 2

106 J. P. Mackey, in *The Christian Experience of God as Trinity*, p53, quotes the Jewish scholar Geza Vermes on this point.

These theological errors have had significant consequences. J. Pelikan, in *The Christian Tradition*, quotes Loofs as follows:

> The transfer of the concept 'Son' to the preexistent Christ is the most significant factor in the pluralistic distortion of the Christian doctrine of God.[107]

Lampe describes how these errors have affected Christians' view of Christ :

> The effects, however, especially in popular piety, have been even more far-reaching .... It is thus the Jesus of the Gospels whom the imagination of the worshipper pictures as pre-existing in heaven and descending to earth. He is pre-existent even in his humanity ... The divine Logos is regarded as the subject of the human experience of Jesus, and, since the Logos is already conceptualised as 'Jesus up in heaven', this means that Jesus becomes a kind of invader from outer space.[108]

Under the doctrine of the 'Eternal Son' the Incarnation is seen as the descent from heaven of some kind of 'superman'. This idea is false, because it violates his humanity, his willingness to subordinate his will to that of God, and his faith. If Jesus did not exercise faith in God in the face of the unknown, how can we? How can Jesus be a true pattern for Christians if he really was omniscient and omnipotent, but just not choosing to exercise his knowledge or power?

Jesus had to be a real and authentic man. The idea of a pre-existent 'God the Son' gives us instead, as Lampe puts it, an 'omnipotent spaceman fighting, as it were, with one hand voluntarily kept behind his back'[109]. As we have already remarked, the idea that Jesus could at some times think and speak like a man, and sometimes like an 'Eternal Son', violates Jesus' essential humanity.

A 'God the Son' would have to be some kind of second rank deity. He would have to have his own personality, different from that of God. He would have to take his being and his direction from God. He would have to be *less than* God, and doing the works of God, not his own works. Lampe comments:

> 'Son' ... suggests a being who is not God himself but who coexists beside God and acts as God's agent ... and the door is opened to the Arian denial

---

107 J. Pelikan, *The Christian Tradition*, p189. He refers to what he calls the 'monstrosities' of the Monophysitic christology in the 'swallowing up' of Christ's individual human nature by the personality and nature of a divine preexistent being.

108 G. Lampe, *God as Spirit*, p136.

109 G. Lampe, *God as Spirit*, p137.

> that the Son or Logos whom men encounter in Jesus is the fullness of deity.[110]

In spite of the formulas of the Council of Constantinople (see Chapter 2), trinitarianism has always had the tendency to lapse into belief in a supreme God ('Father') and a secondary being called 'Son' who is less than fully God but cannot be fully human. Such a 'Son', less than God, more than man, could never be the Saviour whose blood made the perfect sacrifice for sin.

In summary, in their attempt to make Christianity comprehensible to the pagan world, the second century theologians identified Jesus as a pre-existent 'God the Son'. An 'Eternal Son' contradicts scripture, common sense and the gospel.

A 'God the Son' means more than one god

Trinitarians naturally deny that the Trinity is three gods, and say God is 'one God in three Persons'. But the logic of the classical Trinity of three 'Persons' with their own personalities drives the Trinity into tritheism.

If there is an eternally pre-existent 'God the Son' with a different personality in the 'strong' sense of 'person' from the' God the Father', then he must be in some real sense different from his Father[111]. The trinitarian formula of *'one nature, three persons'* does not solve the difficulty, but merely covers it up. The difference between two 'persons' with their own independent personalities is too great to be bridged by saying they have the same nature[112].

Different divine 'persons' in the strong sense effectively mean more than one God. A Trinity of three independent personalities results in tritheism, three gods. This problem has been recognised by some modern theologians; some have rejected the classical Trinity completely and some have tried to re-interpret it.

---

110 G. Lampe, *God as Spirit*, pp139f.

111 See Chapter 1 for the implications of the meaning of 'person' for the doctrine of the Trinity.

112 See Chapter 2 for a discussion on the problems of the 'three in one' formula.

The Trinity cannot explain Jesus' prayer

The Trinity doctrine has several problems with the prayer of Jesus:

1. The doctrine requires Jesus' prayer to be to the First Person of the Trinity, 'the Father'. However Jesus' prayer was to *God*, not a 'First Person'.

2. The Trinity requires Jesus to be both God and man, a 'God-man', who had the personality of the 'God the Son', yet also, because he was a man, could pray validly. But if Jesus had the personality and memory of a 'God the Son' there is no way that his prayer could be anything more than pretence.

3. The Bible shows Jesus continuing in prayer after the Ascension and therefore still human, contrary to the doctrine of the Trinity.

Dealing first with the object of Jesus prayer, note that Jesus prayed to God as a man does. He addressed God as 'my God'. In Chapter 4 it was shown that Jesus uses the terms 'God', 'my God', 'Father', 'the Father', 'my Father' quite interchangeably when he talks about God. There is no distinction between these terms[li]. All refer to God. Jesus *never* talks as a 'God the Son' addressing a 'God the Father'. When Jesus talks about 'the Father' and 'my Father', he is referring to *God himself*, not to a First Person of a Trinity. For instance compare:

I came forth from God ... (John 8:42)

I came forth from the Father ... (John 16:28)

I ascend unto my Father, and your Father: and to my God, and your God (John 20:17)

The trinitarian account of Jesus' prayer therefore falls at the first hurdle. If God were a Trinity, Jesus' prayer would have to have been to the whole Trinity, not just to the First Person.

Secondly, if Jesus were the Second Person, his prayers would have to have been from the Second Person to the whole Triune God, including himself. In other words, Jesus would have been praying to a triunity that included himself. Such 'prayer', if it can be called prayer, could not be authentic prayer. Authentic prayer is from *man* to *God*, from a human to a divine object outside himself. If Jesus had the consciousness that he was 'God the Son', even with powers temporarily laid aside, his prayer could not be authentic. Prayer cannot be between two Persons in the Godhead, even if one of them is temporarily in the body of a man.

The third problem is that Jesus *continues to be a man after the Ascension.* If Jesus had been the 'God the Son' incarnate, then upon his Ascension he would have resumed his rightful place at the right hand of the 'God the Father' and taken his glory back again. If so, then he would not then be able to pray to 'the Father', because a Second Person cannot pray to a First Person. Yet Jesus talks about praying to God after the Ascension. Jesus said:

I will pray the Father and he shall give you another Comforter (John 14:16)

The reference is clearly to the future, after the Ascension. Jesus will be interceding for humanity to God after he is glorified, as scripture indicates[113]:

It is Christ …who is even at the right hand of God, who also maketh intercession for us (Romans 8:34)

But this man, because he continueth for ever, hath an unchangeable priesthood

Wherefore he is able also to save them to the uttermost that come unto God by him, seeing he ever liveth to make intercession for them

(Hebrews 7:24f)

But this man, after he had offered one sacrifice for sins for ever, sat down on the right hand of God (Hebrew 10:12)

According to the Trinity doctrine, the Second Person upon the Ascension puts aside his humanity, takes back his divine privileges and resumes his seat at the right hand of the First Person. This is completely foreign to what the Bible describes. Note that the last verse quoted puts Jesus at the right hand of *God himself*, not a 'First Person'. Furthermore a trinitarian 'Second Person' in heaven could not be the human high priest interceding at the right hand of God.

A 'God the Son' cannot mediate between God and man

According to the classical Trinity, 'God the Son' is a mediator between man and 'God the Father'. There are three problems with this view:

1. 'God the Son', as a co-equal, co-eternal Second Person, could never be a mediator between man and a co-equal First Person. If a First Person needs a mediator, so would a Second Person.

---

113 See also Hebrews 7:17, 8:1, 9:11-14

2. According to the Bible, it is the *man* Christ Jesus is the mediator, not a 'God the Son':

For there is one God, and one mediator between God and man, the man Christ Jesus

(1 Timothy 2:5)

Nowhere in the Bible does it say that a pre-existent divine personage called 'God the Son' is the mediator between man and God.

3. According to the Bible the mediation is between man and *God*, not between man and a 'God the Father'. A trinitarian would really have to say either that mediation is between man and the whole triune God, not just the First Person, or that when Paul (for instance) wrote 'God' he meant the First Person of a Trinity. The first answer raises the problem of how a Second Person can mediate between mankind and all three Persons, including itself. The second answer requires the existence of a 'First Person', which is absent from the Bible. A 'Person' of the Godhead cannot be a mediator either between another member of the Godhead and man, or between the whole triune God and man.

As was stated above, the Bible makes it clear that Jesus *continues in human nature* after Ascension. He is a high priest (Hebrews 2:17, 7:17, 24, 26, 8:1, 9:11, 10:12) and ever lives to intercede (Romans 8:34, Hebrews7:25). Only a man could exercise a priestly role. Furthermore, only the perfect man who died for us can be the perfect high priest:

But this man, because he continueth ever, hath an unchangeable priesthood. Wherefore he is able also to save them to the uttermost that come unto God by him, seeing he ever liveth to make intercession for them. For such an high priest became us, who is holy, harmless, undefiled, separate from sinners, and made higher than the heavens (Hebrews 7:24-26)

The trinitarian claim is that the Atonement needs a Trinity. It is said that three entities are required for a sacrifice: the sacrifice, the one receiving it and the one mediating or offering it. The Son is the sacrifice, offered to the Father, through the Holy Spirit. Trinitarian argument points to such passages as Hebrews 9:14 as proof of this:

... *the blood of Christ, who through the eternal Spirit offered himself without spot to God, purge your conscience from dead works to serve the living God (Hebrews 9:14)*

Notice again that the text, like similar passages, has '... without spot to *God*', not to '*God the Father*' or '*the Father*' used in a trinitarian sense. The Atonement is with *God in his entirety*, not with a 'God the Father' First Person. There are no biblical passages that describe a First Person of a Trinity receiving the sacrifice.

Notice also that it is the '*blood of Christ*' that is the offering, not the blood of a 'God the Son'. Other texts in Hebrews show that it is Jesus Christ *the man* who is both the sacrifice and the high priest. There is no New Testament text that talks about the Atonement in terms of the sacrifice of an 'Eternal Son'. For instance:

By (God's) will we are sanctified through the offering of the body of Jesus Christ ... but this man, after he had offered one sacrifice for sins for ever, sat down on the right hand of God: from henceforth expecting all enemies be made his footstool

(Hebrews 10:10-13, quoting Psalm 110:1)

Jesus Christ the man is the high priest who appears before God and also the sacrifice:

We have such an high priest, who is set on the right hand of the throne of the Majesty in the heavens (Hebrews 8:1)

Christ ... now to appear in the presence of God for us (Hebrews 9:24)

But Christ, being come an high priest of good things to come, ... Neither by the blood of goats and calves, but by his own blood he entered in once into the holy place, having obtained eternal redemption for us (Hebrews 9:11f)

Jesus Christ is still in that holy place, mediating the forgiveness of God by his own blood and interceding for Christians. According to the classical Trinity the ascended Christ is the 'God the Son' who has divested himself of his human nature and taken up again his divine prerogatives. Such a 'God the Son' would have no blood to shed or ability to intercede. A Second Person in the Trinity, an Eternal Son, *cannot* die any more than the First or Third Persons can die.

The Atonement cannot be some kind of transaction between divine 'Persons'. Such a transaction would not deal with the sin of mankind, nor is it described in the Bible. The trinitarian version of the Atonement contradicts the texts that clearly show that both sacrifice and mediator are the glorified human flesh of Jesus Christ, not a 'Second Person'.

The Trinity not solve any problems that are sometimes raised in connection with the Atonement, for instance:

If Jesus died, and Jesus was God, then God died on the cross. But God cannot die.

A possible trinitarian 'solution' is to say that it was only Jesus as God the Son who died, not God the Father. But the principle of 'coinherence' (see Chapter

2) implies the whole of the Trinity is present in any of the Persons, so that if one of the Persons were to die the others would have to undergo the same experience. The paradox of the Cross is that, in Christ, God 'tasted death' (Hebrews 2:9), and yet God cannot die. To say that Christ was 'God the Son' incarnate does not contribute to solving it.

Another possible trinitarian 'solution' is that Jesus was both God and man, and that it was only as man that he died. His divine nature did not die. This answer has even more problems than the one above, because the orthodox doctrine states that Jesus was *one* person with two natures. The difficulties of the trinitarian use of the 'two natures' doctrine are discussed in a separate section below.

In conclusion the Trinity does nothing to explain the Atonement or solve any problems connected with it. The Bible shows that atonement is always made to *God himself*, not a trinitarian 'God the Father'. Jesus Christ *the man* is the perfect sacrifice and the great High Priest. A high priest has to be human in order to intercede. The glorified ascended Christ is still interceding for us with the Father. His blood still pays the debt for our sin.

An 'Eternal Son' cannot be begotten

There are two conflicting views of the Son. The first view is that Jesus Christ is the incarnation of the 'Eternal Son'. The second view is that Jesus Christ had a beginning in time when he was born in Bethlehem. This is a simple alternative. One or the other must be true, and both cannot be true.

The doctrine of the pre-existent Eternal Son originated with the second century Apologists. In the fourth century the doctrine set out at Nicaea declared that the Son is 'co-eternal' with the Father, in order to oppose the Arian idea that Jesus was a created being. 'Co-eternality' means that the Son existed *from the beginning*. The Nicene declaration stated that there was never a time when the Son was not

In line with the Eternal Son doctrine, such sayings of Jesus as *"Glorify thou me ... with the glory which I had with thee before the world was" (John 17:5)* are interpreted by trinitarians in terms of the Eternal Son remembering his past glory. The problem with this interpretation is that it violates Jesus' essential humanity (see above). Nevertheless in this section we will take the Eternal Son doctrine at face value and consider the texts used to support it.

Aside from sayings of Jesus like John 17:5, one of the most important texts used to support the Eternal Son is in Colossians 1[114]:

(The Son) is the image of the invisible God, the firstborn of every creature:

For by him (the Son) were all things created ... all things were created by him, and for him:

And he (the Son) is before all things, and by him all things consist

And he (the Son) is the head of the body, the church: who is the beginning: the firstborn from the dead: that in all things he might have the pre-eminence (Colossians 1:15-18)

In determining how to interpret texts like these, we need to consider the other texts that state the Jesus was born at a moment in time. John's Gospel explicitly declares that Jesus is the only-begotten Son[115]:

... the glory as of the only begotten of the Father ... (John 1:14)

In Galatians it is stated that Jesus is 'made of a woman':

But when the fulness of the time was come, God sent forth his Son, made of a woman, made under the law (Galatians 4:4)

Jesus was born of Mary in Bethlehem by the Holy Spirit:

The Holy Ghost shall come upon thee. And the power of the Highest shall overshadow thee: therefore also that holy thing which shall be born of thee shall be called the Son of God (Luke 1:35)

The birth of Jesus Christ in Bethlehem had been foreseen from the beginning and prophesied in Old Testament times. For instance, it is agreed by most scholars that Psalm 2 is a 'messianic' psalm[lii] that speaks of Jesus Christ, and verse 7 speaks prophetically of his birth[116]:

The Lord hath said unto me, Thou art my son, this day have I begotten thee (Psalm 2:7)

---

114 Other texts often cited in support of the Eternal Son doctrine are Philippians 2:6-9 and Hebrews 1. These are discussed in separate sections below.

115 See also John 1:18, 3: 16, 18. The Greek word *monogenes* translated as 'only-begotten' does not imply that Jesus was God's *only* son, but that he was unique. Mackey, *The Christian Experience of God as Trinity*, p58.

116 Psalm 2:7 is quoted at least five times in the New Testament (Matthew 3:17, Acts 13:33, Hebrews 1:5 and 5:5, 2 Peter 1:17).

For something to be 'begotten' or 'made', there has to be a time when it came into existence, and before which it was not. These biblical statements clearly indicate that 'the Son' had a beginning when Jesus was born of Mary. But they contradict the view that the Son has always existed. How could an Eternal Son be made of a woman? How could an Eternal Son be begotten at a moment of time if he has always existed?

A trinitarian may say in reply that Jesus was *not* actually born at Bethehem. According to the classical Trinity the Son 'descended to earth' at Bethlehem, but was not begotten at that time. Yet a trinitarian would have to agree that the Son was still begotten at *some* time, because the Bible clearly states this. But if the Son was begotten, *when* was he begotten?

Theologians have proposed different solutions to this. Tertullian believed that the Son came into being when God uttered his first word in 'Let there be light'. Origen tried to reconcile the contradictory ideas of the Son being begotten at a moment in time with the Son being eternal with a notion of 'eternal generation', whereby the Son is always being generated. This idea seems a little far-fetched to many.

Another trinitarian argument relies on the 'God-man' concept of Jesus:

The Son is both God and man. As God he was there in the beginning. As man he was born in Bethlehem.

However this answer raises more questions than it settles. It does not answer how Jesus could have a unitary personality, but could remember his life as a man and *also* remember his pre-existent life as the Eternal Son. No authentic human being, still less a perfect one, could have such memories (see below).

How can the texts that appear to suggest pre-existence be better interpreted? First consider Jesus' prayer in John 17 referred to earlier:

And now, O Father, glorify thou me with thine own self with the glory which I had with thee before the world was (John 17:5)

Jesus was not speaking of the glory that an Eternal Son literally had before creation. What glory could that be? The 'glory' of the Son is not that he existed from eternity, but that he died to save mankind. Jesus was speaking of the fore-ordained glory that his coming death would achieve.

Consider how God views time. He is not bound by human constraints.

... one day is with the Lord as a thousand years, and a thousand years as one day (2 Peter 3:8)

God sees all events in time as stretched out before him, past, present and future:

I am God ... declaring the end from the beginning, and from ancient times the things that are not yet done (Isaiah 46: 9-10)

There are many passages in the Bible where God speaks of something to happen in the future, as though it were present now. Furthermore, God sees all history in terms of his redemptive plan. All has been foreseen from the beginning of time. God's plan for the end is to unite all things in Jesus Christ:

That in the dispensation of the fullness of time, he might gather together all things in Christ, both which are in heaven, and which are on earth ... (Ephesians 1:10)

God's plan for mankind is:

to bring many sons unto glory (Hebrews 2:10)

The Book of Revelation speaks of

... the book of life of the Lamb slain from the foundation of the world (Revelation 13:8)

Nobody would interpret this passage as saying that the Lamb was *actually* slain at the foundation of the world [117]. The Lamb was slain at the cross. The passage has to be interpreted in terms of God's plan. In his plan, future events are present already. God sees the death of Christ, the bringing of many sons unto glory and the uniting of all things in Christ as ever-present, even though we see the first event as in the past and the others as future.

God's plan has the death of Christ at its centre. In John 17:5, Jesus speaks of his mission as if it were already accomplished. The glory he had before the foundation of the world was the glory he had in God's plan for the salvation of mankind. Jesus does *not* speak of some *past* glory that he remembers having enjoyed as a pre-existent Eternal Son. He speaks of the glory ever-present to the mind of God that is consummated by Jesus' death and resurrection.

The passage of Colossians 1 passage should be interpreted in the same way, as should the similar passage in Hebrews 1 (see separate below). The pre-existence

---

[117] Although Origen's theory might be extended to talking (absurdly) about the Son *continually being slain.*

of Christ is in the mind and the plan of God, not literally as an Eternal Son. Colossians 1:18 speaks of the Son as 'the beginning'. The Greek word is *arche*, which can mean 'first in line' 'first in authority' 'founding principle' as well as 'first in time'. Colossians 1:15 calls him 'the firstborn of all creation'. In a similar way, that can be translated 'preeminent'. There is no necessity to interpret Colossians 1 in terms of the Eternal Son view.

In conclusion the 'Eternal Son' doctrine is contradictory to scripture. The alternative view that the Sonship literally began with the birth of Jesus in Bethlehem is the correct biblical view. Texts suggesting pre-existence are to be understood prophetically in terms of God's plan. There is no necessity to take such passages to mean that the Son existed before Christ was born.

The two views of the Son of God

The 'Eternal Son'

- **The Son existed from eternity as the co-eternal Second Person**
- **Texts referring to the birth of Jesus cause problems for this view**

This view is unbiblical

The Son had a beginning

- **The Sonship began with Jesus' birth**
- **'Pre-existence of the Son' texts refer to existence in the divine plan**

This is the biblical view

'Sending of the Son' texts

Jesus talked frequently about being 'sent' by God, 'coming' from God and 'coming down from heaven', and the epistles talk in similar terms. For instance:

... *he that receiveth me receiveth him that sent me (Matthew 10:40)*

... *My meat is to do the will of him that sent me, and to finish his work (John 4:34)*

... *He that heareth my word, and believeth on him that sent me, hath everlasting life ... (John 5:24)*

For I came down from heaven, not to do mine own will, but the will of him that sent me (John 6:38)

I came forth from God ... (John 8:42)

I came forth from the Father ... (John 16:28)

As thou hast sent me into the world, even so have I also sent them into the world (John 17:18)

... God sent forth his Son, made of a woman ... (Galatians 4:4)

And we have seen and do testify that the Father sent the Son to be the Saviour of the world (1 John 4:14)

We can understand Jesus coming from heaven without the meaning of a literal descent of a 'God the Son'. The Bible speaks about a man 'sent' from God in terms of *prophetic call* or *commissioning*, for instance:

There was a man sent from God, whose name was John (John 1:6)

Clearly John the Baptist did not literally descend from heaven.

John 17:18 confirms that the 'sending from God' of which Jesus speaks is the same sense in which the disciples are sent. This cannot be the sending of a pre-existent being from heaven, but must be 'sending' in the sense of commissioning.

A trinitarian would say is that the Son (the Second Person) was sent from heaven by the Father (the First Person). However the sending of the Son was not a First Person sending a Second Person, but the sending of the man Jesus Christ by God. As has already been noted, the New Testament makes no distinction between 'God' and 'the Father'. There is no trinitarian 'Father' in the New Testament. 'Father' refers to God in his entirety. Jesus spoke of coming from 'God' and coming from 'the Father' in the same sense. For instance compare:

I came forth from God ... (John 8:42) and *I came forth from the Father ... (John 16:28)*

The two passages have identical meaning. 'God' and 'the Father' have the same reference. It would be difficult to argue that the sending of John 8:42 was from the whole Trinity but that the sending of John 16:28 was just from the First Person.

Consider again John 6:38:

I came down from heaven, not to do mine own will, but the will of him who sent me

Who sent Jesus? It can only be the same as in John 8:42 and 16:28, in other words God in his entirety and not a First Person of a Trinity.

Consider again Galatians 4:4:

... God sent forth his Son, made of a woman ...

A literal interpretation is self-contradictory. A 'God the Son' sent from 'God the Father' could not be made of a woman.

The Sonship began in time at the birth of Jesus in Bethlehem. The only correct way to interpret texts that speak of Jesus being sent by God or coming down from heaven is in terms of the commissioning of the only-begotten Son of God, not the descent from heaven of a pre-existent heavenly Eternal Son.

'Creation by the Son' texts

According to the Trinity, 'God the Son', created the universe on behalf of 'God the Father'. Texts such as John 1:3, 1:10, 1 Corinthians 8:6, Ephesians 3:9, Colossians 1:16f, and Hebrews 1:2 are used to support this.

It has already been shown that the doctrine of the 'Eternal Son' is unbiblical. When God created the universe he did not need any other person's help to do it. He created by his Word. He spoke and it was. There is no necessity to imply or conclude that God's Word has a separate personal existence, from God, or from any 'God the Father'. The texts that are used to support the idea of creation by an 'Eternal Son' should be interpreted in the same way as 'sending of the Son' texts, that is in terms of the eternal plan of God.

The Prologue to John's Gospel is an important passage for the Trinity, and is worthy of a separate discussion (see below). But the main points to note are that John 1:1-3 do not mention Jesus or the Son at all, but are about the Word of God. The Word is the agent of creation, not the Son. It is the Word that was in the beginning with God, not Jesus Christ. Jesus Christ, the Son of God, is the Word *made flesh*, and not referred to at all in this passage.

In the passages from the epistles of Paul and the Letter to the Hebrews, there is a different emphasis. The emphasis is on the Son of God and his place in the divine plan. Here are the main texts:

the cosmic plan of God to unite all things in Christ (Ephesians 1:10)

... there is but one God, the Father, of whom are all things, and we in him: and one Lord Jesus Christ, by whom are all things, and we by him (1 Corinthians 8:6)

... the fellowship of the mystery, which from the beginning of the world hath been hid in God, who created all things by Jesus Christ (Ephesians 3:9)

For by him (the Son) were all things created, that are in heaven, and that are in earth, visible and invisible, whether they be thrones or dominions, or principalities or powers: all things were created by him, and for him. And he is before all things, and by him all things consist (Colossians 1:16-17)

(God) hath in these last days spoken unto us by his Son, whom he hath appointed heir of all things, by whom also he made the worlds (Hebrews 1:2)

These passages speak of the role of the Son of God in the wider plan of God, made from the beginning, to unite all things in Christ (Ephesians 1:10). The term 'Son of God' refers to Jesus Christ, the man born of Mary, not to an 'Eternal Son' (see above in this chapter). Notice also that 1 Corinthians 8:6 and Ephesians 3:9 describe creation as by *Jesus Christ*, not an 'Eternal Son'.

Turning to Colossians 1 and Hebrews 1, it would be difficult to argue that 'Son' in Colossians 1 and Hebrews 1 refers to an 'Eternal Son' but that 1 Corinthians 8:6 and Ephesians 3:9 have a *different reference*, to Jesus Christ. This would give inconsistent interpretations to similar texts. Consider the Greek words translated 'by' (KJV) in these passages. In Colossians 1:16 the Greek is literally 'because *in* him all things were created'. The Greek preposition *ev*, normally translated 'in', has a number of possible meanings, including 'in respect of', on occasion of', 'on the ground of'[118]. Later in the same verse the preposition *dia* is used. This is also translated 'by' in the KJV, and can mean 'by means of'. However it can also mean 'on account of', 'because of', 'for the sake of', 'with a view to'. A similar argument and interpretation applies to Hebrews 1:2, where the word translated 'by' is *dia.*

In conclusion, 'the Son' should be interpreted consistently throughout the New Testament as 'Jesus Christ, the Son of God'. The Son of God, Jesus Christ, is the centre of the eternal plan of God. The man Jesus Christ, the Saviour of the world, is the reference point for both the beginning and the end of history.

John's Gospel talks about creation by 'the Word of God' not by Jesus Christ. Paul's letters and Hebrews speak of the world being 'made by the Son' in the sense that when God created the world he had the plan for redemption by Jesus Christ in mind.

---

[118] *Analytical Greek Lexicon*, Samuel Bagster and Sons, London 1973.

'Son at the right hand of the Father' texts

A trinitarian may point to the New Testament texts that describe the glorified ascended Christ in heaven at the right hand of God (or of power) as proof of at least two divine persons. This argument is superficially appealing, but false. Certainly there are many texts that describe 'two in heaven', but this does not prove the Trinity. The 'two' are God and the ascended Lord Jesus Christ, not two divine persons.

Let us examine the 'two in heaven' texts in detail. Many, if not all, of them are quotes from or possible references to the 'messianic' Psalm 110:

The Lord said unto my Lord, Sit thou at my right hand, until I make thine enemies thy footstool (Psalm 110:1)

Some of the New Testament texts that allude to or quote Psalm 110:1 are:

Hereafter shall ye see the Son of man sitting on the right hand of power ... (Jesus in Matthew 26:64 cf Mark 14:62 and Luke 22:69)

Therefore being by the right hand of God exalted, ... (Peter in Acts 2:33, going on to quote Psalm 110:1 in v34f)

Behold, I see the heavens opened, and the Son of man standing on the right hand of God (Stephen in Acts 7:56)

Which he wrought in Christ, when he raised him from the dead, and set him at his own right hand in the heavenly places (Ephesians 1:20)

Wherefore God also hath highly exalted him, and given him a name which is above every name (Philippians 2:9)

... seek those things which are above, where Christ sitteth on the right hand of God (Colossians 3:1)

... when he (God's Son) had by himself purged our sins, sat down on the right hand of the Majesty on high (Hebrews 1:3)

But to which of the angels said he at any time, Sit on my right hand, until I make thine enemies thy footstool? (Hebrews 1:13)

Seeing then we have a great high priest, that is passed into the heavens, Jesus the Son of God ... (Hebrews 4:14)

Wherefore he is able to save them to the uttermost that come unto God by him, seeing he ever liveth to make intercession for them (Hebrews 7:26)

... we have such an high priest, who is set on the right hand of the throne of the Majesty in the heavens (Hebrews 8:1)

Looking unto Jesus, the author and finisher of our faith: who for the joy that was set before him endured the cross, despising the shame, and is set down at the right hand of the throne of God (Hebrews 12:2)

... by the resurrection of Jesus Christ: who is gone into heaven, and is on the right hand of God (1 Peter 3:10)

The first difficulty with the trinitarian interpretation of these passages is that (as was pointed out in Chapter 1) none of these texts mention the Holy Spirit. Only *two* in heaven are described, not three.

The second and principal objection to the trinitarian interpretation is that the two in heaven are never described as two divine persons. In all the texts he who is on the right hand of the throne of God is quite clearly the ascended Jesus Christ. He is the man who died for us and is now the great High Priest, continually making intercession for us. A Second Person of a Trinity cannot make intercession for humanity (see above). The only one who can do this is the one who died for us and whose blood redeemed us, Jesus Christ the Son of God.

Jesus Christ is still continuing in his priestly intercessory role until his work is done. 1 Corinthians 15:23-25 tells of a time when his work will be done (again referring to Psalm 110:1):

... Then cometh the end, when he shall have delivered up the kingdom to God, even the Father: when he shall have put down all rule and authority and power. For he must reign till he hath put all enemies under his feet (1 Corinthians 15:24f)

The end of the Sonship shall be when all enemies are put under his feet, and the work of the Son in redemption is completed.

The 'two in heaven' passages therefore provide no evidence for a 'God the Son'

John 1:1-3 and 1 John 1:1-2

This section examines John 1:1-3 and 1 John 1:1-2. They are important sources for trinitarian doctrine because they are the only texts where trinitarian argument can find Jesus is described in terms of 'the Word'. However the contexts make clear that Jesus is the Word of God *made flesh*, not a pre-existent divine person. There is no 'Eternal Son' described as being in the beginning with a 'God the Father'. It is *the Word* that is in the beginning with *God himself*, not one divine Person together with another divine Person.

Consider first John1:1-3:

In the beginning was the Word, and the Word was with God, and the Word was God (John 1:1)

The same was in the beginning with God (John 1:2)

All things were made by him: and without him was not anything made that was made (John 1:3)

A trinitarian would interpret this passage as stating that Jesus Christ, as 'God the Son', the Second Person in the Trinity, was in the beginning with 'God the Father', the First Person. Furthermore the passage is interpreted as saying that 'God the Son' created the world on behalf of 'God the Father'. This interpretation is out of context with that of the gospel as a whole. The emphasis in the gospel is on the Word *made flesh*. Jesus Christ was a man of flesh and blood. His miracles were the 'signs' that Jesus did, so that we might believe that he is the Messiah (John 20:30f). The final sign was his physical resurrection, for which physical evidence was required. Not only Thomas, but all the disciples saw his hands and side (John 20:20). The gospel is not about some pre-existent 'God the Son', but about the man Jesus Christ, the only begotten Son.

There are three specific points to make in rebutting the trinitarian interpretation:

1. 'The Word of God' is not a divine person

2. John 1:1-3 do not mention Jesus or some person called 'the Son'

3. John 1:1-3 put 'the Word' as separate from God himself, not a 'God the Father'

The Word of God is not a person

In Chapter 3 we pointed out the error in assuming that an attribute of God must be a divine person because the Bible speaks of it sometimes in a personal way. In the Old Testament 'Word', 'Wisdom', 'Spirit' are described in personal terms as a poetic device. This does not provide a valid reason for inferring that 'Word', 'Wisdom' and 'Spirit' really are different divine persons.

In ordinary speech the 'word' of someone is never understood to mean a separate person from that person. On the contrary, ordinary language use often *identifies* a person and his word. For instance where a ruler's word is obeyed, it is as if the ruler is present in person. 'The word' of somebody has no 'personality' beyond the personality of the person whose word it is. It would be nonsense to talk of 'the word of Peter' as a separate person from Peter, and it makes no sense even to describe it as a 'personally distinct way' (to use trinitarian language) in which Peter exists. 'The word of Peter' is just what Peter says or has said. The same reasoning should apply to the Word of God. There is no biblical evidence for concluding that the Word of God has an independent personality from God (or a 'God the Father')[119].

A trinitarian could point out the use of the personal pronoun 'him' in verse 3 as proof that the Word is a person. However this is just a matter of Greek grammar. The Greek term *Logos* is masculine, therefore pronouns applied to it are also masculine (e.g. 'he', 'him' and 'whom') rather than neuter (e.g. 'it' and 'which'). The same would apply to any noun of masculine gender. The use of 'him' in English translation does not prove that the Word is a person.[120]

The writer of John's Gospel inherited the *Logos* terminology from Greek philosophy and the interpretation that the Jew Philo had made in terms of 'the Word of God' in the Old Testament. There was no implication in this use that the *Logos* had a personality of its own. It was only later much that Christian theologians, beginning with Irenaeus, called it 'the Son' and attributed personality to it. It was later still that trinitarian theologians called it 'the Eternal Son' and interpreted Jesus' words as those of the Eternal Son.

---

119 A similar argument applies to talk of the Spirit of God. Genesis 1:2 speaks of the spirit of God moving on the face of the waters. However, nobody would conclude from that statement that God's spirit must therefore be a different person from God (See Chapters 1 and 6).

120 See Chapter 6 for a similar point in respect of the Spirit.

The Word of God is the subject of John 1:1-3, not Jesus or 'the Son'

The terms used are 'Word' (Greek *logos*) and 'God' (Greek *theos*). The phrases 'the Son', 'God the Son' and 'God the Father' do not appear in the passage[liii]. 'God the Son' is not a biblical term at all. The term 'God the Father' is always used in the Bible as a synonym for God in His entirety, and never to distinguish a First Person from the other Persons of a Trinity (see Chapter 4).

The name 'Jesus' does not appear in the passage. Jesus Christ is the Word incarnate, made flesh, and does not make an appearance until verse 14. The subject in verses 1-3 is quite clearly 'the Word'. There is no implication here that 'the Word' is a separate person from some other person called 'God the Father'. Still less is there the implication that 'the Word' is the same as some divine person called 'the Son'. Even less is there the implication that 'the Word' is a person who shares the personality of the man Jesus who was born in Bethlehem.

When verse 10 refers to the world being made *by him* the reference is to the Light, or the Word, with which God created the universe and that lights every man. Again, there is no necessity to conclude that the passage speaks of two persons present at creation.

Trinitarian teaching routinely assumes that 'the Word' is a direct reference to Jesus Christ the man, and there is often no attempt to justify that assumption. For instance, Stephen Davey, in his *Wisdom for the Heart* publication on John 1:1-3 states:

> In John 1:2 we are also told that Christ was 'in the beginning with God'. In other words, Jesus Christ existed before time again. He was, as theologians refer to it, pre-existent.[121]

There is no justification for assuming 'the Word' in John 1:1-3 refers to Jesus Christ. Jesus Christ is not mentioned until John 1:14, and he is the Word *made flesh.*

---

[121] Stephen Davey, *Wisdom Journal 1*, p10. See also the quote from Radio Bible Class below.

John 1:1 says the Word was with *God* not a 'God the Father'

A common trinitarian argument is to quote *'the Word was with God'* and point out that the Greek (*pros ton theon*) means 'over against', implying separateness. The conclusion is drawn that 'the Son' was 'distinct' from 'the Father' in the beginning, and so there must be two divine persons. For instance, the tract *Who is this man who says he's God?* from Radio Bible Class Ministries, quotes John 1:1 and states:

> *'The Word was with God'* This clause indicates that although Jesus was God, He was a distinct entity who had, as the preposition *with* implies, communion and fellowship with God the Father.[122]

The trinitarian assumption that 'the Word' refers to Jesus has already been noted. Now notice that the term 'God the Father' has been introduced instead of 'God', making the assumption that there *is* such a being as a 'God the Father'. This assumption is not justified.

In fact John 1:1 does not put a Second Person 'God the Son' face to face with a 'God the Father'. It places 'the Word' face to face with *God*, not a First Person. If the trinitarian interpretation were correct and 'was with God' means distinct personal existence, then it would show that the Word has a distinct personal existence from *God himself*. This would result in a being called 'the Word' who is divine, but less than fully God. The consequence of the trinitarian interpretation of John 1:1-3 is not a 'God the Son' who is fully God, but a secondary deity.

The correct interpretation of John 1:1-3 is that 'the Word' has no separate personal existence from God. In the process of creation God's Word was with God. There is no implication of two distinct divine Persons.

The Prologue to John's Gospel: John 1:1-3

- **'The Word of God' is not a person**
- **'The Word' is the subject, not Jesus Christ**
- **'The Word of God' is with God himself, not with a 'God the Father'**

122 RBC Ministries, *Who is this man who says he is God?*, p13.

Turning to 1 John 1, the correct interpretation is the same as for John 1:1-3. The emphasis in the First Letter of John, as with John's Gospel, is on the fact that Jesus came *in the flesh*. The letter is not about the pre-existent Eternal Son of the Trinity, but about the man Jesus Christ who is the *manifestation* of the Word of God. For example the letter emphasizes that the spirit of antichrist is distinguished from the spirit of God by its denial that Jesus Christ has come *in the flesh* (1 John 4:2f). It is the *manifestation* of the Son of God that will destroy the works of the devil (1 John 3:8). An Eternal Son does not deliver from evil.

Trinitarian argument cites the first two verses of the letter as proof that Jesus was in the beginning with 'God the Father'. However the true meaning taken in context is quite different from the trinitarian interpretation:

That which was from the beginning, which we have heard, which we have seen with our eyes, which we have looked upon, and our hands have handled, of the Word of life.

(For the life was manifested, and we have seen it, and bear witness, and shew unto you that eternal life, which was with the Father, and was manifested unto us;)

That which we have seen and heard declare we unto you, that ye also may have fellowship with us: and truly our fellowship is with the Father, and with his Son Jesus Christ.

(1 John 1:1-3)

These verses say the same as John 1:1-2, 9 and 1:14 but in slightly different language. The 'eternal life which was with the Father' is the Word of God. It is, as John 1:9 puts it, the true Light that lights every man. However this 'eternal life' is not a person in its own right, but an attribute of God.

When the 'eternal life' was manifested, the Word became flesh in the form of Jesus Christ, and the author bears witness to it. But Jesus Christ himself was not there in the beginning.

Philippians 2: did the Son descend from heaven?

Philippians 2:5-11 is a well-known text that is often cited as support for the Eternal Son doctrine. Believed to incorporate an early Christian hymn, it has been interpreted as describing the supposed 'self-emptying' of 'God the Son' when he descended to earth:

Let this mind be in you, which was also in Christ Jesus

Who, being in the form of God, thought it not robbery to be equal with God

But made himself of no reputation, and took upon him the form of a servant, and was made in the likeness of men

And being found in fashion as a man, he humbled himself, and became obedient unto death, even the death of the cross.

Wherefore God also hath highly exalted him, and given him a name which is above every name

That at the name of Jesus every knee should bow, of things in heaven and things in earth, and things under the earth

And that every tongue should confess that Jesus Christ is Lord, to the glory of God the Father

(Philippians 2:5-11)

A related text is 2 Corinthians 8:9:

for ye know the grace of our Lord Jesus Christ, that, though he was rich, yet for your sakes he became poor, that ye through his poverty might be rich. (2 Corinthians 8:9)

The trinitarian interpretation[123] of these passages is that 'God the Son' was rich in the sense of enjoying heavenly glory before his incarnation as Jesus Christ. The word 'being' (Greek *huparchon*) in verse 6 is interpreted to mean 'eternally existing'[124]. He then 'became poor', 'made himself of no reputation' and 'humbled himself' by becoming man. Upon his ascension he resumed his rightful place in heaven and took back his glory. The trinitarian understands Paul to be exhorting the Philippians to have an attitude like that of the Eternal Son.

Yet this is an unnatural interpretation of the passage. Can one seriously understand Paul to be asking the Philippians to put themselves in the place of an 'Eternal Son' putting aside his heavenly glory and coming to earth? Paul is talking about the attitude of *Christ Jesus, the man.* In fact the term 'Son' does not occur in the passage. If Paul had been talking about an 'Eternal Son' he would have indicated it more clearly.

---

[123] It is called a 'kenotic' interpretation from the Greek *kenosis* meaning 'self-emptying'.

[124] This point was made by a trinitarian representative at the John Ankerberg debate, J. Ankerberg et al, 1985. In fact, *huparchon* is the ordinary participle for 'being' and carries no implication of eternal existence.

Rather than being about the mind of an Eternal Son, the passage is much more naturally interpreted in terms of Paul urging the Philippians to have the mind of Christ, the man. Jesus humbled himself. He did the will of his Father in heaven. The example of humility and obedience presented by the life of Jesus Christ on earth is an example that we can follow. Notice again the reference to 'God' himself in verse 9, not a 'God the Father'. It was *God* who exalted *Jesus* (verse 10).

J. P. Mackey, in *The Christian Experience of God as Trinity*, quotes the work of Schillebeeckx on this passage and comes to a similar conclusion. Pointing out that the text does not use the title 'Son' at all, he goes on:

> Now there is no doubt about the fact that, as Schillebeeckx maintains, this hymn is its present form can be quite adequately and intelligibly interpreted in terms of 1. Genesis 1:26, where God makes man in his own image and likeness; 2. Psalm 8:4-6, about making man a little less than the *elohim*; 3. Jewish theology of the king as 'the man' or 'the Adam' and even member, with the angels, of the heavenly court and 4. The suffering servant material from Deutero-Isaiah. From this background the subject of the hymn, Jesus, though Messiah, did not grasp at the exalted status of the *elohim*, but was born and 'found' as an ordinary mortal, the slave of those angelic powers which envied man and/or ruled the world, and being just this ordinary man, quite empty of that exalted status of the kingly sons of God, he then humbled himself to the very death of a criminal slave on a cross. Therefore, God exalted *Jesus*: no pre-existent divine figure resumed its original status.[125]

These two passages, and other similar ones, are not about a 'God the Son' who left heaven and assumed mortality. They are about Jesus Christ *the man*, who, although the Son of God and able to call upon legions of angels, was content to live a life of obedience, service and sacrifice.

Hebrews 1: does the Father call the Son 'God'?

Hebrews Chapter 1 is another important source for trinitarianism. Not only does it begin with statements that are used to support 'creation by the Son', but it contains what appear to be clear statements that the Son is God, but a different person from 'the Father'. Hebrews 1:8 reads:

But unto the Son he saith, Thy throne, O God, is for ever and ever ... (Hebrews 1:8)

[125] J. P. Mackey, *The Christian Experience of God as Trinity*, pp61-62.

A common trinitarian argument uses this to say that:

Hebrews 1:8 shows the Father calling the Son 'O God'. If the Father can call the Son 'God' then the Son must be a divine Second Person.

Not only that, but a trinitarian may also use Hebrews 1:8 to explain why the Son can call the Father 'God' and still be God:

If the Father can call the Son 'God' and still be God, then the Son can call the Father 'my God' or 'God' and still be God.

A correct interpretation of Hebrews 1:8 does *not* show 'the Father' addressing 'the Son' as 'God'. First of all consider the context. The theme of the Letter to the Hebrews is Jesus Christ, the Son of God, the great High Priest. The emphasis is on the *humanity* of the Son, not his supposed deity. It is not possible for a divine 'Second Person' to stand in the gap between God and man, to be a high priest or to intercede for his brethren (see Hebrews 2:17, 7:24-28, 8:1-6). It is not possible for an immortal 'Eternal Son' to shed his blood to take away our sin (Hebrews 9:14).

Chapter 1 introduces the letter. The subject is Jesus Christ the Son of God, the Word of God made flesh. Note again that 'Son' in verse 2 is the Son of God himself (verse 1), and not the Son of a 'First Person'.

The author begins by asserting that the Son is the reason and the heir of creation, higher than angels, the visible image of God. Verse 2 ... *by whom (the Son) also he (God) made the worlds* describes creation being on account of Jesus Christ, rather than a Second Person being present at the time (see above in this chapter).

The author proceeds to describe the nature of the Son and his progress to God's right hand:

Who being the brightness of his glory, and the express image of his person, and upholding all things by the word of his power, when he had by himself purged our sins, sat down on the right hand of the Majesty on high (Hebrews 1:3)

The first half of the verse describes the Son in similar language to that in John 1:14. Jesus Christ is the manifestation of God in human form, the 'Word made flesh'. The second half is one of the many New Testament passages that show the ascended Christ at the right hand of God. These passages do *not* describe an 'Eternal Son' returning to a place that he occupied before.

The nature of the Son as 'so much better than the angels' is now described in more detail. The epistle was written to Jews, and so the author makes his argument by quotations from the Old Testament, using Psalms 2, 45, 97(perhaps), 102, 104, 110 and 2 Samuel 7. The references are given in square brackets.

Being made so much better than the angels, as he hath by inheritance obtained a much more excellent name than they.

For unto which of the angels said he at any time, Thou art my son, this day have I begotten thee? [Psalm 2:7]

And again, I will be to him a Father, and he shall be to me a Son? [2 Samuel 7:14]

And again, when he bringeth the first begotten into the world, he saith, And let all the angels of God worship him [Psalm 97:7?]

And of the angels he saith, Who maketh his angels spirits, and his ministers a flame of fire [Psalm 104:4]

But unto the Son he saith, Thy throne, O God, is for ever and ever, a sceptre of righteousness is the sceptre of thy kingdom [Psalm 45:6]

Thou hast loved righteousness, and hated iniquity: therefore God, thy God, hath anointed thee with the oil of gladness above thy fellows [Psalm 45:7]

And, Thou, Lord, in the beginning hast laid the foundation of the earth: and the heavens are the works of thine hands [Psalm 102:25]

They shall perish; but thou remainest: and they shall all wax old as doth a garment [Psalm 102:26]

And as a vesture shalt thou fold them up, they shall be changed: but thou art the same, and thy years shall not fail [Psalm 102:27]

But to which of the angels said he at any time, Sit on my right hand, until I make thine enemies thy footstool? [Psalm 110:1]

(Hebrews 1:4-13)

Verse 4 states that Son was *made* so much better than the angels. This again emphasizes the humanity of the Son. See also Galatians 4:4, where the Son is described as 'made of a woman, made under the law'.

Turning to verses 5-13, the writer is adducing evidence from the Old Testament for the divine origin of the Son, but also for his humanity and his nature as a *begotten* son. The Son can be seen from two perspectives. From God's perspective, the Son is His begotten (v5), his anointed (v9) and raised to his right hand (v13). But from the point of view of humanity, the Son is addressed as God (v8, v10), because he is the express image of God (v3) and God's representative on earth. Note that Psalm 45 is a so-called 'royal' psalm, addressed to the king of Israel. The kings of Israel were regarded as God's representatives on earth.

Consider now the trinitarian argument that the Father appears to call the Son 'God' in verse 8:

1) The biblical contrast is between *God* and the Son, not 'the Father' and the Son. There is no trinitarian 'God the Father' in Hebrews 1, or anywhere else in the New Testament. Therefore the first half of the 'Father-Son' pairing needed by the trinitarian argument is missing.

2) In verse 8 *he saith* (NIV *he says*) is interpolated by the translator. It is not there in the Greek. The verse does not quote God calling the Son 'God'.

3) Verses 8 and 9 are a direct quotation from Psalm 45:6f. Psalm 45 is classified by scholars as a 'royal' psalm addressed to the king, God's anointed. In Psalm 45:6 the king appears to be addressed as 'O God' (Hebrew *Elohim*), but the whole context of the psalm is an address to the king *from his people*. How could an earthly king be addressed as God? The original Hebrew is literally 'Your throne God (*Elohim*) for ever and ever'. Bible scholars have given a number of different interpretations of this verse, only one of which has the traditional interpretation that the King is being addressed as *Elohim*[liv]. However, even under this interpretation, *Elohim* sometimes refers to a mighty man, a godlike being or as God's representative[126]. This fits the context of Psalm 45 well. The Messianic ruler, seen by his people, is the face of God, God's representative on earth. The king is blessed by God (verse 2) and anointed by God (verse 7, see next point). Verse 6 shows him appointed with divine authority as God's representative. Therefore the context shows that it is not God calling the ruler 'O God', but *the people*. The people of Israel do not commit the sin of making a man into God, but they address the king as God's representative.

4) The person addressed in Psalm 45, the Messianic ruler, is a *man* and not God. Psalm 45:7 reproduced in Hebrews 1:9 states that:

---

[126] See e.g. Exodus 4:16 and 7:1

Thou hast loved righteousness, and hated iniquity: therefore God, thy God, hath anointed thee with the oil of gladness above thy fellows (Psalm 45:7/Hebrews 1:9)

The subject of this verse is the Son (Hebrews) or the Messianic ruler (Psalm 45). It refers to 'God, thy God', making it clear that God is the God of the Son (Messianic ruler), and so emphasizing his humanity. Only a human can be anointed. Only a *man* can have men as 'fellows'. Hebrews 2:17 calls humanity the Son's 'brethren'.

Humans may worship Jesus as Lord of Lords and address him as 'God' without forgetting that he is also a man who also addressed God as 'God' while on earth. But God himself never calls Jesus 'God'.

In conclusion Hebrews 1 gives a portrait of the Son of God, seen from different perspectives as God's begotten and anointed and as the face and image of God to men. But it does not show two divine Persons 'God the Father' and 'God the Son'.

Trinitarian argument: 'The Son is both God and man'

This familiar trinitarian argument could be summarized as:

The Son is both God and man, one person with two natures.

As man he was born in Bethlehem, could pray to the Father, could address the Father as 'my God' and die on the Cross.

As God, he was the incarnation of the Second Person of the Trinity who laid aside his heavenly privileges to come to earth.

As the Second Person he could speak about his intimate relationship with the First Person.

The trinitarian claim is that because Jesus is God and man, he can be an authentic human being while also being 'God the Son'. For instance Bowman, in *The Biblical Basis for the Doctrine of the Trinity*, states that:

> Jesus calls the Father "My God" because He is still man as well as God[127]

---

[127] R.M. Bowman, *The Biblical Basis of the Doctrine of the Trinity*, p9.

The argument relies heavily upon the 'two natures' doctrine set out in the fourth century Declaration of Chalcedon (see Chapter 2). This stated that Jesus Christ was fully God and also fully man: one person with two natures, human and divine.

The Chalcedon statement was formulated to safeguard both Christ's deity and his individual humanity from 'heresies' such as Adoptionism, Arianism and Sabellianism. It was not an explanation of how Christ could be both God and man, but an attempt to exclude what were believed to be heretical views: on one extreme that Christ was not an individual and complete human being and on the other extreme that Christ was not fully God.

The trinitarian position makes use of the 'two natures' view of Christ to claim that the doctrines of the Incarnation and the Trinity support each other. Gregory Boyd, in *Oneness Pentecostals and the Trinity*, states that:

> ... the Incarnation and the Trinity go hand in hand[128]

Boyd answers the question how Jesus can refer to the Father as *his* God:

> On the face of it, the traditional trinitarian answer to this differs little from the answer Oneness believers would themselves give; namely, it is because of Christ's Incarnation, because of the fact that he was a full human being, that he could not only refer to the Father as *his* God, but also explicitly say that the Father was greater than he (John 14:28). It was, moreover, for this same reason that the Son had to continually pray to God as any human must pray[129]

Boyd, in arguing against the oneness pentecostal view (as he understands it) that the divine nature of Jesus is the Father and that Christ may be seen as sometimes taking the part and place of God and sometimes that of man, goes on to assert that only the Trinity can explain the Incarnation:

> However we trinitarians differ radically from Oneness Pentecostals in the way we maintain this truth ... the Incarnation mean that *everything* Christ went through and did, God went through and did ... The one person of Jesus Christ cannot be split into two ... Hence, when Christ suffered, God suffered ... and when Christ suffered a forsaken death, God suffered a forsaken death ... The Oneness insistence that it was not God, but only as a man, that Christ did these things splits Christ in two and is tantamount to denying the Incarnation altogether! ... Only a belief that God can and does fully exist in

---

[128] G. Boyd, *Oneness Pentecostals and the Trinity*, p66.

[129] G. Boyd, *Oneness Pentecostals and the Trinity*, p58.

more than way - trinitarianism - can truly affirm that God could really become a man without thereby depleting his own infinite transcendence.[130]

Boyd is surely correct that Christ cannot 'be split into two'. And most would agree that God went through everything Christ did (2 Corinthians 5:19). But the trinitarian explanation in terms of 'two natures' is not a true explanation at all. In fact it runs the same risk of destroying the integrity of Jesus' personality that Boyd accuses oneness pentecostalism of.

The main problem with the trinitarian use of the 'two natures' doctrine is that it requires Jesus to have the personality of 'God the Son' as well as having the personality of a complete and authentic human being. As was pointed out earlier in this chapter, it requires Jesus to be speaking with the memory of the 'God the Son' when he talks about being sent by the Father (e.g. John 6:38) and the glory he had with the Father in the beginning (John 17:5).

The supposed strength of trinitarianism is that it can account for sayings of Jesus like John 6:38 and 17:5. However this interpretation means that Jesus must be speaking sometimes as God the Son and sometimes as man, and therefore cannot be an authentic human being (see above in this chapter). No authentic human being can remember his existence as a pre-existent divine 'Person', and *be correct about it.* If a person were to claim he had memory of a life before he was born, we would send for psychiatrists. *Genuine human beings do not have previous existences.*

A trinitarian may perhaps say that these problems do not apply, because 'God the Son' is voluntarily choosing not to exercise his divine privileges and powers while on earth. Even so (according to the Trinity) 'God the Son' is still *aware* of his divine status, and can still *remember* his past heavenly glory (see e.g. John 8:58 and John 17:5), even if he is not exercising his divine powers. Therefore the problem remains.

Boyd does seem at one point to acknowledge the problem. If Jesus is *at some times* speaking as 'God the Son', for instance when he says 'I came down from heaven' (John 6:38), and *at other times* just a man (as when he prays or talks of God as 'my God'), then, as Boyd points out, this 'makes out Jesus to be someone with a multiple personality disorder'[131]. However nothing that Boyd

---

[130] G. Boyd, *Oneness Pentecostals and the Trinity*, pp58f

[131] G. Boyd, *Oneness Pentecostals and the Trinity*, p88.

says here actually addresses the issue. If the Jesus of the oneness pentecostals has a personality disorder (according to Boyd) because he speaks sometimes as God and sometimes as man, then the Jesus of the Trinity equally has a personality disorder because he speaks sometimes as 'God the Son' and sometimes as man. There is no relevant difference between the two positions.

Boyd claims that it is the supposed fact that God can exist in more than one way that solves the problem. But this is not so. The number of 'Persons' in the Godhead is irrelevant to the issue of how an individual man can be the incarnation and have the personality of one of these 'Persons' and still remain an authentic human being. The real issue is about what it is to be *a genuine human being*, not about whether God exists in more than one personally distinct way.

The 'two natures' doctrine can provide no explanation as to how Jesus can be both an authentic human being and also have the personality of a 'God the Son'. In fact, as we have pointed out, the doctrine of 'two natures' was not an explanation at all, but an attempt to exclude extremes that were thought heretical. To say that Jesus was a 'God-man' explains nothing.

The doctrine of the Trinity needs Jesus to have the personality of the 'God the Son' *as well as* the personality of a complete, authentic and sane human being. But no sane human being can remember his existence before he was born. If Jesus were an authentic human being, it would be *impossible* for him to think and speak as God, even on rare occasions, because that would violate his humanity. The only solution is to recognise that Jesus thought and spoke like a man at all times. There was no time when he thought or spoke as a 'God the Son'.

In conclusion, to cite the 'two natures' doctrine in order to explain how Jesus could pray validly and still be 'God the Son' explains nothing, but exposes the shaky foundations of the classical doctrine of the Trinity. The supposed strength of the doctrine was that it could identify the earthly life of Jesus with that of a 'God the Son' who came down from heaven, who has the memories, will and so on of this 'God the Son' and whose relationship with 'the Father' is a continuation of a relationship between two co-eternal 'Persons'. This supposed strength turns out to be a fatal weakness.

Conclusions

The doctrine of the Eternal Son is the centrepiece of the classical Trinity. However it is inconsistent with the Bible and incompatible with the humanity of Jesus. The 'Eternal Son' needs a 'God the Father', and neither can be found in the Bible.

A 'God the Son' with his own independent personality violates monotheism. The trinitarian formula of 'three persons with one nature' is only able to hide this fact by the use of an elastic definition of 'person'. If 'person' means only a personal way in which God manifests himself, then some kind of trinitarian concept of God might be biblical. However the classical Trinity needs three 'Persons' in the strong sense, meaning independent personalities with their own centres of consciousness, wills and memories. This effectively means more than one god. These problems with the Trinity explain the attempts of theologians in recent times to redefine or revise the doctrine.

We pointed out three principal ways in which the 'Eternal Son' doctrine is unbiblical. An 'Eternal Son' cannot pray authentically, cannot be a mediator between God and man and cannot have been 'made of a woman' as the Bible requires. The trinitarian argument that Jesus could do these things because he was both God and man is an inadequate explanation. For Jesus to be fully human, he had to have thought and spoke as a man *at all times*. The idea that he could have on some occasions thought and spoke as a man and at other occasions as 'God the Son' violates his essential humanity.

The trinitarian is forced to the conclusion that Jesus must speak at least on *some* occasions as 'God the Son' because he believes that Jesus is the incarnation of 'God the Son' and so has the personality of a pre-existent being. Statements of Jesus like *"I came down from heaven, not to do mine own will, but the will of him who sent me" (John 6:38)* and *"Glorify thou me ... with the glory which I had with thee before the world was" (John 17:5)* are interpreted as those of 'God the Son' speaking. But it is impossible for Jesus to have had the personality of a 'God the Son' when he spoke John 6:38 and 17:5 and also to be an authentic human being. The trinitarian use of the 'two natures' doctrine does not solve the problem but rather covers it up.

Finally, the scriptural texts which are used to 'prove' the doctrine of the Eternal Son, such as those speaking about 'creation by the Son' or 'the Son coming down from heaven', are shown to be capable of interpretation in terms of Jesus

Christ the begotten Son of God, the Word of God made flesh, who was born of Mary in Bethlehem.

The doctrine of 'God the Son' or the 'Eternal Son'

- **A 'God the Son' cannot be found in the Bible**
- **A 'God the Son' violates monotheism**
- **A 'God the Son' cannot pray authentically**
- **A 'God the Son' cannot be a mediator between God and man**
- **An 'Eternal Son' could not be begotten**
- **Texts used to support pre-existence of, descent of, or creation by the Eternal Son can be interpreted in terms of Jesus Christ the begotten Son of God**
- **'Two in heaven' texts show the glorified Christ at the right hand of God, not a 'God the Son' with a 'God the Father'**
- **Trinitarian explanations in terms of 'two natures' are unsuccessful**

6. THE MISSING THIRD PERSON

A 'Third Person' of a Trinity cannot be found in the Bible

The Holy Spirit is personal but that does not make it a 'Person'

The 'Cinderella' of the Trinity

Many trinitarians would admit, if being honest, that it is difficult to find a clear statement in scripture that the Holy Spirit is a Third Person in the Godhead. There is in fact little real scriptural evidence that the Spirit has a personality independent from another person called 'the Father'.

Even it were accepted that there is a 'God the Father' and a 'God the Son', questions can be asked about the so-called 'God the Spirit':

How much can the Spirit be distinguished from God Himself?

Is the Spirit another mediator between God and man, alongside the Son, but perhaps of less importance? If so, why do we need another mediator?

How much biblical evidence is there for supposing there is a 'God the Spirit' who is a separate personality from a 'God the Father'?

Does the Spirit really have a personality of its/his own, or is it/he just the anointing, the power and the presence of God?

If the Spirit does have a personality of his own, how come he never says anything of himself, but only what he hears from the Father (John 16:13)?

Why do we never hear what the Spirit himself thinks?

The problem of the 'Third Person' is in some ways the opposite to that of the 'Second Person'. There is no difficulty distinguishing the Son from the Father, while there is a problem with the Son being co-eternal and equally divine with the Father[132]. There is no difficulty in seeing the Spirit as divine and eternal, while there is a problem *distinguishing* the Spirit from God.[133].

---

[132] For instance the Son said 'my Father is greater than I' (John 14:28). See Chapter 5.

[133] J.P. Mackey comments that 'grave problems are encountered in any attempt to distinguish Spirit from the God who is named as Father', *The Christian Experience of God as Trinity*, p66

The belief that the Holy Spirit is a 'Third Person', with its or his own personality, is often seen as an afterthought to the more central doctrines of the Trinity. Alister McGrath, in *Christian Theology: An Introduction*, describes the Holy Spirit as having long been 'the Cinderella of the Trinity. The other two sisters may have gone to the theological ball; the Holy Spirit got left behind every time'[134]. McGrath remarks that, with the rise of the charismatic and pentecostal movement, the Spirit is no longer a 'Cinderella'. The new experience of the reality and power of the Spirit in the church has had an impact on theology. Yet to have a renewed interest in the Spirit is not the same as believing that it is the Third Person of Trinity. For instance, oneness pentecostals deny the Trinity completely[135] and nobody could accuse pentecostals of being uninterested in the Spirit.

Historically the Spirit was admitted into the Godhead as an equal member later than the first two 'Persons' and only because it was felt necessary to protect 'the Son' from the possibility of being a divine being of lower rank than 'the Father'. Despite being supposedly of equal rank to the Father and the Son, the Spirit has had a rather indeterminate status both in trinitarian theology and in the popular mind.

Historical development of the 'Third Person' doctrine

In Old Testament times the term 'Spirit' (Hebrew *ruach*, meaning 'breath' or 'wind') was used to describe an attribute of God. Like the terms 'Wisdom' and 'Word', 'Spirit' is one of what Geoffrey Lampe describes as 'bridge' terms, which express the idea of God's outreach towards, and contact with, the created world.[136] These terms may sometimes be described in personal terms, for instance Wisdom in Proverbs 8. This is a poetical device known as the 'personification of intermediaries' (see Chapter 1). However there is no evidence that the Jews thought that 'Wisdom', 'Word' and 'Spirit' really were separate personalities in the Godhead.

In the second century the Christian Apologists formulated the idea of a divine 'Logos' (Greek for 'Word') that soon became identified as a pre-existent 'Son' and was seen as having the personality of Jesus Christ. The theology of the Apologists was primarily binitarian, with a Supreme God and the divine Logos.

---

134 A. McGrath, *Christian Theology: An Introduction*, p279.

135 D. Bernard comments that the doctrine of the Holy Spirit is the weakest link in the doctrine of the Trinity, *The Oneness of God*, pp127-130.

136 G. Lampe, *God as Spirit*, p35.

The Logos was the mediator between God and man. At this time there was no clear distinction between 'Word' and 'Spirit' (Greek *pneuma*). Both terms were used to refer to this divine mediator.

However once the Logos became identified with the pre-existent 'Son', then 'Spirit' lost the place it once had in Christian theology as a term for the mediator between God and man. There was a further complication because the term *pneuma* had been used in a rather materialistic sense by the Stoic philosophy. Lampe describes the downgrading of the Spirit:

> 'Spirit', which could not be directly identified in the same way with the concrete historical person of Jesus Christ, but only with the more abstract concept of his divinity, was thus gradually detached from its old association with 'Wisdom' and 'Logos', and was superseded, in what became orthodox Christology, by 'Logos-Son' as the way of expressing the outreach of God to men in Jesus ... The Spirit of God tended in this way to be relegated to the status of a second or extra mediator between God and man, occupying the third place, inferior and subordinate to the pre-existent Son, as a somewhat hazily conceptualized 'power' or 'grace' ... and reduced in meaning from a way of speaking about God in his activity to a name for a third, and something like an extra, divine hypostasis (meaning person) ... [137]

Thus, by the end of the second century AD, the Spirit was reduced to 'third place' and a rather uncertain status within the Godhead. So it has remained.

The identification of the Spirit as a third co-equal 'Person' came late on. Earlier trinitarian theologians such as Tertullian and Origen claimed divinity for the Holy Spirit, but both put the Spirit in third place after the Father and the Son. Tertullian was the first to use the formulae of three *personae* in one substance. However the view that the Spirit is a person in his own right and of the same 'rank' as the Father and Son, co-eternal with both, was not articulated until the Council of Constantinople in 381 AD.

The Father and the Son had been officially 'members' of the Godhead since the Council of Nicaea in AD 325, of equal rank and having the same nature (Greek *homoousios*). After Nicaea the founding theologians of the Trinity were under pressure from Arianism. They were concerned to defend the 'same nature' definition that the Son has the same nature as the Father and that both are divine co-eternal persons. But if the Spirit could be a subordinate divine person

---

[137] G. Lampe, *God as Spirit*, pp33-135.

of lower rank than the Father (as some were saying) then why not the Son as well?

The trinitarian theologians believed that the Holy Spirit had to have the same status as the Son in order to protect the full divinity of the Son. They therefore felt obliged to regard the Spirit as having the same nature as the Son and the Father, as a third co-equal member of the Godhead. The Holy Spirit came into the Godhead 'on the coat tails', as it were, of the Son.

Biblical evidence for the 'Third Person'

In the Old Testament, the term 'Spirit' (when referring to the Spirit of God) was sometimes used in a personal way. However, as we have already stated, that cannot be taken as evidence that the Spirit of God is an independent personality within the Godhead. In most cases, the Spirit of God is God's presence, God's influence and God's enabling power.

Consider for example Genesis 1:1-3, one of the important reference texts for the Trinity doctrine. Genesis 1:2 describes the 'spirit of God moving on the face of the water'. That does not prove independent personality for the Spirit. It just shows that God created the world by his Spirit.

Furthermore, Genesis does not mention any person called 'God the Father'. God himself does the creating. If the Spirit (and the Word) is a separate person involved in creation, it/he must be separate from *God himself.* If the Spirit is a divine person it or he must be a separate being from God and inferior to God, contrary to the doctrine of the Trinity.

In the New Testament 'Spirit' is used in the same sense as the Old Testament, particularly in Luke's Gospel and Acts. In Acts, there is however a new dimension added. The Holy Spirit is now the *gift* of God to all Christian believers, as shown in Peter's speech at Pentecost

Then Peter said unto them, Repent, and be baptized everyone of you in the name of Jesus Christ for the remission of sins, and ye shall receive the gift of the Holy Ghost (Acts 2:38)

In Acts, the gift of the Spirit is evidenced by speaking in tongues (Acts 8, 10 and 19), but opinions differ as to whether the Spirit can be received *without* speaking in tongues.

In the Letters of Paul, a new personal element and a new doctrinal emphasis is given. The Spirit is none other than the 'Spirit of Christ', which is the same in turn as 'the Spirit of God', and it is necessary for salvation. Consider the well known passage from Romans 8:9-11:

But ye are not in the flesh, but in the Spirit, if so be that the Spirit of God dwell in you. Now if any man have not the Spirit of Christ, he is none of his.

And if Christ be in you ...

But if the Spirit of him that raised up Jesus from the dead dwell in you, he that raised up Christ from the dead shall also quicken your mortal bodies by his Spirit that dwelleth in you (Romans 8:9-11)

There is no difference for Paul between the reference of the terms 'the Spirit', 'the Spirit of Christ', 'the Spirit of God' and 'Christ'. The terms mean the same. The Spirit is the same as the indwelling Christ. The Holy Spirit is now not just a gift to accompany salvation, it is the presence of Christ in the believer and it is essential for salvation. Notice also that there is no distinction made between the presence of Christ and the presence of God. A believer does not experience three Persons; he experiences just *one* person, God in Christ.

In fact there is little real evidence in the New Testament for a 'God the Spirit'. We have already remarked on the fact that, although God and Jesus Christ are mentioned together numerous times in the New Testament, there is *no occasion in which all three Persons of the Trinity are described together.* For instance all the greetings in the epistles are from God and Jesus Christ, never from all three Persons. Similarly scenes in heaven (e.g. Acts 7:56, Revelation 4-5) describe God and Christ with no mention of the Holy Spirit[lv].

John 1:1-3 is much cited as proof of the pre-existence of Jesus. Yet the Spirit is not mentioned in the passage[lvi]. The Letter to the Colossians, an important source for trinitarian doctrine, contains no mention of the Holy Spirit at all.

J. P. Mackey concludes his examination of New Testament texts as follows:

> In short, most of the spirit-material in the New Testament is christology. It is concerned, that is to say, to give expression to the status and function of Jesus of Nazareth, God's anointed one. It is not in the least concerned to give us any substantial information about a divine 'person' or *hypostasis* distinct both from Jesus Christ and the God he called Father.[138]

---

[138] J.P. Mackey, *The Christian Experience of God as Trinity*, p86.

Despite the lack of any extensive evidence for the 'Third Person' in the New Testament, trinitarian advocates make the case for it, citing in particular John chapters 14-16. In the next section we will examine the trinitarian argument in detail.

Trinitarian argument for the 'Third Person'

Trinitarians may believe that the case for a 'Third Person' is straightforward and uncontroversial. Because the Spirit is a) divine and b) personal it must follow that the Spirit is a Third Person in the Godhead.

The first step, that the Holy Spirit is divine, is fairly uncontroversial. Thus, Ankerberg and Weldon, in *The Personality and Deity of the Holy Spirit*, argue for the deity of the Spirit:

> The Holy Spirit is deity because He performs the functions of God and because He is called God in scripture. He has the attributes of deity, such as omnipresence (Psalm 139:7); omniscience (1 Corinthians 2:10f); eternality (Hebrews 9:14); omnipotence (Job 33:4). And He gives eternal life (John 3:3-8). He is also the Creator (Job 33:4; Genesis 1:2) ... It is also clear from Scripture that the Holy Spirit is God by the divine functions that he performs and by the divine associations that He has ... The Holy Spirit is also called God. In Acts 5:3-4, the one lied to is first said to be the Holy Spirit, who is then immediately identified as God. He is called 'the Lord' in 2 Corinthians 3:18 and in Hebrews 10:15-16 ... [139]

It is also clear that the Spirit has personal characteristics. It can for instance be grieved (Ephesians 4:30) Sometimes trinitarians give the impression that this is all that is needed to prove that there is a Third Person.

In fact the argument for a 'Third Person' involves several steps:

(1) The Holy Spirit is divine

(2) The Holy Spirit is personal therefore a Person

(3) The Father is the First Person in the Godhead

(4) The Holy Spirit is not identical to the Father

therefore

---

[139] J. Ankerberg and J. Weldon, *The Personality and Deity of the Holy Spirit*, p2.

(5) The Holy Spirit is another Person in the Godhead

Even if one accepted the third and fourth steps, the argument fails because the second step cannot be justified logically or scripturally.

'Personal' does not imply a Person

Trinitarians often assume that because the Spirit is personal it must be a 'Person'. The Holy Spirit is the Spirit of God. Therefore it clearly has personal characteristics. But that does not prove that it is a 'Person' in its own right, with a centre of consciousness, personality, will,.emotions and memory, separate and distinguishable from other 'Persons'.in the Godhead.

Similarly, we may speak about 'the spirit of a man' in personal terms, but that is no argument for concluding that the spirit of man has a separate personality from that man.

The trinitarian case makes heavy use of John 14-16 because of the use of the personal pronouns 'he', 'him', 'whom' etc. for the Spirit in those texts. Here are some of the main passages:

And I will pray the Father, and he shall give you another Comforter that he may abide with you for ever;

Even the Spirit of truth: whom the world cannot receive, because it seeth him not, neither knoweth him: but ye know him: for he dwelleth with you, and shall be in you.

I will not leave you comfortless: I will come to you. (John 14:16-18)

If a man love me, he will keep my words: and my Father will love him, and we will come unto him, and make our abode with him. (John 14:23)

But the Comforter, which is the Holy Ghost, whom the Father will send in my name, he shall teach you all things, and bring all things to your remembrance, whatsoever I have said unto you (John 14:26)

But when the Comforter is come, whom I will send unto you from the Father, even the Spirit of truth, which proceedeth from the Father, he shall testify of me: (John 15:26)

... It is expedient for you that I go away: for if I go not away, the Comforter will not come unto you: but if I depart, I will send him unto you. (John 16:7)

Howbeit when he, the Spirit of truth is come, he will guide you into all truth: for he shall not speak of himself: but whatsoever he shall hear, that shall he speak: and he will shew you things to come.

He shall glorify me: for he shall receive of mine, and shall shew it unto you. (John16:13f)

As stated above, the use of the personal pronouns 'he', 'him', 'whom' is often cited as proof that the Holy Spirit is a person in his (or its) own right. However their use in John 14-16 is simply a matter of Greek grammar. Personal pronouns applied to the Spirit prove nothing.

In John 14-16 the Holy Spirit is described as the 'Comforter', translating the Greek *parakletos*, a masculine noun. It therefore requires the use of masculine personal pronouns to refer to it, because in Greek (like Latin, French, German, Italian and Spanish) the gender of the pronoun agrees with the gender of the noun. In the original Greek there is no implication that *parakletos* is a person, any more than for instance house, bread or fruit (also masculine nouns in Greek) are people.

Wherever the word 'Spirit' is used, in Greek *pneuma*, a neuter noun, the pronouns used in the Greek are neuter (English 'which', 'it' etc.). For instance in the first half of John 14:17, the Spirit is described as 'the Spirit of truth'. The Greek pronouns standing for the Spirit in the next clause are *o*, meaning 'which' and *auto*, meaning 'it', and these are so translated in literal translations. A literal KJV-style translation of the Greek should read:

Even the Spirit of truth; ***which*** *the world cannot receive, because it (the world) seeth* ***it*** *not* ...

(John 14:17)

A footnote on these two pronouns in John 14:17 given in the *Zondervan Parallel New Testament* reads:

> The gender of these pronouns agrees, of course, with the antecedent *pneuma* (neuter); and this has been kept though the personal Spirit of God is meant. Elsewhere, masculine pronouns are in fact used.[140]

The translators of the Parallel New Testament have translated the Greek literally, but are aware of the presumptions of bible translators. Assuming that the Spirit is a person, the KJV and NIV translate *o* as 'whom' and *auto* as 'him'. Thus the KJV reads:

Even the Spirit of truth; ***whom*** *the world cannot receive, because it (the world) seeth* ***him*** *not ... (John 14:17)*

The translators have deliberately changed the gender of the pronouns, because of their belief that the Spirit is a person. However the beliefs of translators

---

[140] *The Zondervan Parallel New Testament in Greek and English*, The Zondervan Corporation, Grand Rapids, Michigan, USA, 1980.

should not determine matters of biblical truth. The genders of personal pronouns prove nothing about whether or not the Holy Spirit is a person.

More on the 'Third Person'

Trinitarian argument also cites the saying of Jesus that 'we' will come to the believer as proof of the 'threeness' of God and the personhood of the Holy Spirit.

If a man love me, he will keep my words: and my Father will love him, and we will come unto him, and make our abode with him (John 14:23)

A trinitarian would understand the 'we' as meaning 'we three persons of the Trinity'. This is understandable, especially given the context. The discourse in John 14-16 talks about the 'Comforter' for the first time, and teaches that the Spirit will be given to believers and will dwell in them. However that Jesus did not say 'we three'. In fact he does not mention the Spirit at all in verse 23. He is talking about himself and God coming to dwell in the believer. It is significant that, even in the passages that are most cited as proof of the Trinity and of the personhood of the Holy Spirit, there is no reference to God being three persons, three person dwelling in the believer, and so on.

There is no necessity to interpret the 'we' of John 14:23 in terms of three divine persons. 'We' can be understood as the Spirit of Christ living in the believer, which is God, in Christ, in us. Notice that Jesus describes this indwelling elsewhere in the same discourse as *I in them, and thou in me ... (John 17:23)*. This is why Jesus also describes the 'we' in the believer as 'I' in John 14:18. The 'we' in 14:23 living in the believer is not three divine persons, but the Spirit of Christ, which is the same as the Spirit of God (Romans 8:9-11).

Another point for discussion is the seeming lack of personality of the Spirit. The Spirit does what it is told and speaks what it is told to say. For instance see: *Howbeit, when he*[141]*, the Spirit of truth, is come, he will guide you into all truth: for he shall not speak of himself: but whatsoever he shall hear, that shall he speak: and he will shew you things to come. (John 16:13)*

The Spirit just speaks what it receives from God. How could the Spirit then be co-equal, or even a separate personality, if it acts as a mere instrument of God? Just in the case of 'Word', 'Spirit' is an attribute of God or a mode of God's self-expression. The Spirit is never shown in the Bible as a separate personality.

---

141 In the Greek there is no word for 'he' throughout this verse. The translation could equally well read 'it'.

His 'personality' is the personality of God. The Spirit indwelling the believer has the personality of God *in Christ.*

I in them, and thou in me ... (John 17:23)

Conclusions

There is no biblical evidence for seeing the Spirit as having a personality of its own. Both Old and New Testaments talk of the Spirit of God without any implication that it is a separate personality from God. It is a mode of God's self-expression. It has personality, but the personality is that of God. Just as the spirit of a man is not a separate being from that man, so the Spirit of God is not a separate personality from God.

Furthermore the argument for the Third Person would never be made without the prior acceptance of the First and the Second Persons. When those are taken away, the need for a Third Person disappears.

Conclusions concerning 'God the Spirit'

- **'God the Spirit' is the weakest link in the Trinity doctrine**
- **The Bible does not show that the Spirit is a separate person**
- **The Spirit indwelling the believer is 'God in Christ in us', not a 'God the Spirit'**

7. BEYOND A TRINITY

The doctrine of the classical Trinity fails to uphold monotheism, explain the deity of Christ or account for the relationship between God and Christ

The doctrine has resulted in tritheistic tendencies and uncertainty about who Jesus is

The doctrine has resulted in poor understanding of Christianity by Judaism and Islam

The doctrine should be replaced by the understanding that the one God is revealed through Christ and the Spirit

The Trinity doctrine today

The orthodox doctrine of a 'classical' Trinity sees God as a society of three co-eternal co-equal Persons with their own centers of consciousness and personalities. 'Mainstream' denominations regard those who question the doctrine as heretics or unbelievers. But it is no longer possible to claim that the Trinity doctrine has universal assent and that those Christians who question it are outside the true Church for three reasons.

Firstly, it is by no means clear that all Christians belonging to trinitarian denominations really believe in or even understand the doctrine. Many (including many ministers) say 'It is a mystery' and leave it at that. The implication of having a half-understood doctrine at the centre of the faith are discussed below.

Secondly, the classical doctrine is not accepted by theologians. Some have said that the traditional language is outmoded and that the doctrine, if it is to be relevant in modern times, needs to be restated in different terms. Others have rejected the doctrine altogether.

Thirdly there are significant numbers worldwide of openly non-trinitarian Christian individuals and organisations.

The failures of the Trinity doctrine

Chapter 1 stated three fundamental beliefs, the varying degrees of assent to which lie behind the doctrinal disputes of the last two thousand years

- **God is one (meaning monotheism)**
- **Jesus Christ is God**
- **There is a difference between God and Jesus**

The apostolic church worshipped Jesus as God. Yet Jesus was not the same as the God he called 'Father'. So there seem to be more than one god. The doctrine of the classical Trinity claims to 'solve' these problems by affirming all three beliefs with the formula:

God is three persons in one nature

However, as we have seen, the doctrine of the classical Trinity does not provide convincing accounts for any of these three beliefs.

In the first place the classical Trinity violates monotheism. The doctrine has to bear the weight of accounting for a Father and a Son with separate centres of consciousness and personalities, because the trinitarian view of Jesus requires him to have the personality of an Eternal 'God the Son'. In practical terms this means two separate beings. Trinitarians understandably say that they believe in only one God. Yet the logic of the trinitarian position leads inevitably towards more than one divine being[lvii].

In the second place, the trinitarian 'explanation' of the deity of Christ in terms of the 'two natures' is full of difficulty. The supposed strength of the Trinity is being able to account for such sayings of Jesus as:

"I came down from heaven, not to do mine own will, but the will of him who sent me"

(John 6:38)

"Glorify thou me ... with the glory which I had with thee before the world was" (John 17:5)

in terms of the 'God the Son' talking. However this results in a Jesus who talks at one time with the consciousness and memory of a 'God the Son' and at other times with the consciousness and memory of a man. Such a Jesus cannot be a complete, authentic and perfect man, but either a hybrid half-man half-God or else some kind of superbeing who is only pretending to be human.

The doctrine of the Incarnation is often described as a 'divine mystery' (1 Timothy 3:16). Trinitarians like Gregory Boyd say 'the Incarnation and the Trinity go hand in hand'[142], and claim that the Trinity can explain how Jesus can be fully God and fully man. In fact the Trinity doctrine does nothing to explain the Incarnation, but instead requires Jesus to be something different from an authentic human being. If the Incarnation is a divine mystery, the Trinity adds to it a 'man-made' mystery about which the Bible says nothing.

In the third place there is a problem for the Trinity in accounting for the distinction between God and Jesus; trinitarians consider this the strong point of the doctrine. The problem is that the relationship between God and Jesus is always a relationship between *God and man*, never between two divine 'Persons'. The biblical Jesus Christ is the only begotten Son of God, the man who came into physical existence at Bethlehem. There is no such person as an 'Eternal Son'. Jesus had to think and speak as a man at all times, if he was a genuine man.

We have also shown how the classical Trinity contradicts the Bible. The supposed 'threeness' of God cannot be found anywhere in scripture, and key 'trinitarian' texts do not support a Trinity. The trinitarian 'God the Father', 'God the Son' and 'God the Spirit' were shown to have no biblical foundation.

Three failures of the classical Trinity

- **The Trinity violates monotheism**
- **The Trinity cannot explain how Jesus can be God**
- **The Trinity cannot account for the relationship between God and Jesus**

The consequences of the Trinity doctrine

The result of belief in the classical Trinity is a Christian faith that is less than biblical and gives a misleading image of Christianity to people of other faiths. This has had three consequences.

[142] G. Boyd, *Oneness Pentecostals and the Trinity*, p66.

The first consequence of the Trinity is that popular Christian faith has become confused between monotheism and tritheism. To believe in three divine 'Persons' comes close to belief in three divine beings. Ordinary Christians cannot be expected to understand the fine distinctions between 'person' and 'being'. This is especially so given the confusion over the definition of 'Person' in the doctrine of the Trinity. If preachers cannot explain how God can be one and also three, how can a Christian explain it to non-Christians? How many 'Persons' are there in the believer? How many voices can the believer hear - three, one (the whole Trinity talking), or four (each 'Person' individually plus the whole Trinity)[lviii]. How many 'Persons' will the believer see in heaven - three or two or one? Trinitarian theology provides no answers to these questions.

The second consequence of the Trinity is a tendency to lapse into a view of Jesus as a semi-divine superhuman, neither properly human nor completely divine. People pray to the Father through Jesus Christ (as the Bible commands), but are unclear how many Persons they are praying to. Is Christ a mediator between man and God, or is he God himself, or both? Do we pray just to the Father, or to the whole Trinity? If the Father is the one that we pray to, is not the Father the 'real' God, and the Son and the Spirit just mediators and second-rank deities? Trinitarian theology gives no satisfactory answer.

The third consequence of the Trinity is the inadequate understanding of Christianity on the part of adherents of other religions, particularly Judaism and Islam. To the strongly monotheistic Jews and Muslims the Trinity doctrine is generally regarded as either tritheistic or incomprehensible (or both), and in contradiction to their sacred scriptures.

Why did Christianity lose out to Islam in vast areas of the former Roman Empire? It has been noted by historians that the roots of Christianity in North Africa in particular were extremely shallow, allowing the almost complete obliteration of indigenous Christianity after the Muslim conquests of the seventh century. Regions like North Africa and Asia Minor (modern Turkey) are today almost devoid of Christianity. The Catholic theologian Hans Kung notes that:

> A main cause of the failure of Christianity seems to have lain in the inadequate foundation of the dogmas of Christology and the Trinity. The Catholic theologian Hermann Stieglecker ... rightly regards this lack as one of the most serious causes of the collapse of Christianity, particularly in its

> homelands, in the Near East and North Africa. It was in fact simpler to believe in the One God and Muhammad, the Prophet after Jesus.[143]

It can fairly be said that the claim of Islam to be the authentic worldwide successor of Judaism and Christianity lies partly in the prominence it gives to its *tawhid* (doctrine of the oneness of God) and its belief that Christianity has betrayed the monotheism of the Old Testament. If Christianity were widely perceived to be as firmly monotheistic as Judaism then this claim of Islam would be much weakened. The doctrine of the Trinity remains today a barrier that prevents Jews and Muslims gaining a correct understanding of the Christian faith.

Three consequences of the classical Trinity

- **Confusion between monotheism and tritheism**
- **Confusion about Jesus - man, God, or half man and half God?**
- **Barrier to understanding of Christianity by Jews and Muslims**

Beyond the Trinity doctrine

The classical Trinity talks of the Persons being co-equal, but the Bible says that 'the Father' is clearly the Person in charge. 'The Son' does the will of the Father, the Son says 'my Father is greater than I', the Son is sent by the Father, begotten by the Father, the Spirit is sent by the Father. Theologians from Augustine have tried to reconcile these two notions; co-equality in the Godhead and subordination of the other Persons to the Father, and have failed. Attempts to define the classical Trinity without subordination only lead to subordination coming back in through the 'back door'.

If the classical Trinity must be rejected, can anything of the Trinity be salvaged? Perhaps, but only by being prepared to set aside the dogma of three co-eternal 'Persons'. In particular it means discarding the doctrine of the 'Eternal Son'.

If it is accepted that 'the Father' is God himself, and not a First Person of a Trinity, then it can be seen that 'the Son' and 'the Spirit' cannot be 'Persons' with their own personalities without making them second-rank deities. So the

143 Hans Kung, *Christianity: Essence, History and Future*, Continuum, New York, 1995, p343

only viable kind of 'Trinity' is an 'economic' view where the Word of God and the Spirit of God are understood in terms of attributes of God which are manifested in personal ways, not as eternal 'Persons'.

Alister McGrath sees the Trinity in the Bible as follows:

> ... the foundations of the doctrine of the Trinity are to be found in the pervasive pattern of divine activity to which the New Testament bears witness. The Father is revealed in Christ through the Spirit. There is the closest of connections between the Father, Son, and Spirit in the New Testament writings. Time after time, New Testament passages link together these three elements as part of a greater whole. The totality of God's saving presence and power can only, it would seem, be expressed by involving all three elements ...[144]

McGrath is talking about the *activity* of God, the presence of God, in the church. It is of course true that 'the Father is revealed in Christ through the Spirit', but we can understand this better as *God* is revealed in Christ through the Spirit. Passages like 1 Corinthians 12:4-6 show that it is *God*, who is revealed in Christ through the Spirit, not a First Person. There is no implication in these passages that Jesus and the Holy Spirit are co-equal and co-eternal divine Persons. For the Apostle Paul, at least, there is no difference between the Spirit and the indwelling Christ.

The trinitarian statements about God manifesting in 'three elements' (McGrath) or 'three personal ways of existing' (Boyd) are really truths about God manifesting himself in *two* ways, not three. So-called 'trinitarian' verses do not show three Persons, but describe the one God working through Christ and the Spirit. There could be common ground between trinitarian and non-trinitarian views on the 'plurality' of God, provided it is understood that

'The Father' is God himself, not a First Person

'The Son' is Jesus Christ, the only begotten Son of God, the Word made flesh, born at Bethlehem, not an Eternal Son

'The Spirit' is the manifestation and the power of God in Christ, not a Third Person

There is undoubtedly much truth in trinitarian statements about God at work in different personal ways. However this truth needs to be rescued from the dogma of the classical Trinity. The Bible shows that the one God reveals

---

144 A.E. McGrath, *Christian Theology: An Introduction*, p293.

himself through Christ and the Spirit. But scripture does not show God to be a Trinity of three co-eternal divine 'Persons'.

Conclusions

- **The classical Trinity violates monotheism**
- **The Trinity doctrine cannot be found in the Bible**
- **The Trinity cannot explain the deity of Christ**
- **The Trinity cannot explain the relationship between God and Christ**
- **The Trinity has led to confusion about who Jesus is**
- **The Trinity has led to a false image of Christianity**
- **The one God manifests himself through Christ and his Spirit, but not as a Trinity**

REFERENCES

J. Ankerberg & J. Weldon, *The Personality and Deity of the Holy Spirit*, Ankerberg Theological Research Institute, USA, 2003 [www.johnankerberg.org].

J. Ankerberg, with C. Beisner, W. Martin, R Sabin & N. Urshan, *Debate on the doctrines of the United Pentecostal Church*, audio cassette, The John Ankerberg Show, Tennessee, USA, 1985 [www.johnankerberg.org].

S. Altaf, *Jeshua or Isa: The True Path for Salvation*, Abrahamic-Faith Ministries, London, 2005 [www.abrahamic-faith.com].

Associated Bible Students, *The Doctrine of Christ*, Clawson, MI, USA, 1997 [www.bibletoday.com].

D.K. Bernard, *The Oneness of God*, Word Aflame Press, Hazelwood, Missouri, USA, 2000.

D.K. Bernard, *Oneness and Trinity A.D. 100 - 300*, Word Aflame Press, Hazelwood, Missouri, USA, 1991.

R.M. Bowman, *The Biblical Basis of the Doctrine of the Trinity*, The Center for Biblical Apologetics, 2004, reproduced in The Blue Letter Bible, 2004.

G. A. Boyd, O*neness Pentecostals and the Trinity*, Baker Book House, Grand Rapids, Michigan, USA, 1992.

H. Chadwick, *The Early Church*, Penguin, 1967.

O. Chadwick, *The Reformation*, Penguin, London, 1964.

S. Davey, *When Heaven Came Down*, Wisdom Journal 1, N. Carolina, 2001.

F.J. Ewart, *The Name and the Book*, Word Aflame Press, Hazelwood, Missouri USA, reprinted 1986 (originally published 1936).

J. Fieldsend, C. Hill, W. Riggans, J.C.P. Smith, F. Wright (eds.), *Roots and Branches: Explorations into the Jewish Context of the Christian Faith*, PWM Trust, Bedford, 1998.

M.H. Graeser, J.A. Lynn, J.W. Schoenheit, *One God and One Lord: Reconsidering the Cornerstone of the Christian Faith*, 3rd edition, Christian Educational Services, Indianapolis USA, 2003.

J.G. Griffiths, *Triads and Trinity*, University of Wales Press, Cardiff, 1996.

N. Gumbel, *Is the Trinity Unbiblical, Unbelievable and Irrelevant?*, Kingsway, Eastbourne, 2002.

G. Lampe, *God as Spirit*, 2nd edition, SCM Press, London, 1983.

J. MacArthur Jr, *Found: God's Will*, 2nd edition, Victor Books, SP Publications, Colorado, 1977.

A.E. McGrath, *Christian Theology: An Introduction*, 2nd edition, Blackwell, 1997.

A.E. McGrath, *The Christian Theology Reader*, 2nd edition, Blackwell, 2001.

J.P. Mackey, *The Christian Experience of God as Trinity*, SCM, London, 1983.

J. Macquarrie, *Principles of Christian Theology*, SCM, London, 1977.

H.R. Mackintosh, *The Doctrine of the Person of Jesus Christ*, T & T Clark, Edinburgh, 1912.

J. Pelikan, *The Christian Tradition: A History of the Development of Doctrine Volume 1*, University of Chicago Press, Chicago, 1971.

Radio Bible Class Ministries, *Who is this man who says he is God?*, RBC, Grand Rapids, Michigan, 2000.

Karl Rahner, *The Trinity*, Heider and Heider, New York, 1970.

Alan Richardson and John Bowden, *A New Dictionary of Christian Theology*, SCM Press, London, 1983.

John A.T. Robinson, *But that I can't believe!*, Collins, London, 1967.

A.W. Wainwright, *The Trinity in the New Testament*, S.P.C.K., London, 1962.

R. Williams, *On Christian Theology*, Blackwell, Oxford, 2000.

N.T. Wright, *Jesus and the Identity of God*, in *Ex Auditu*, 1998, 14, pp42-56 [www.ntwrightpage.com].

ENDNOTES

---

[i] Michael Servetus, who wrote *De Trinitaris erroribus* (1531) and *Dialogues on the Trinity* (1532), was condemned by the Inquisition as a heretic. However he was condemned to death and burnt at the stake, not by the Catholic Church, but by the authorities in Protestant Geneva with the approval of Calvin (Owen Chadwick, *The Reformation*, pp198f).

[ii] Matt Slick, webmaster of CARM, the Christian apologetics internet site, quoted in an e-mail to the author: 'If you are oneness and deny the Trinity, you are not in the faith ... you are outside the body' (26 Nov 2002). ' If you deny the Trinity, you deny the true God' (27 Nov 2002). Adherence to the Trinity is often used as the sole criterion of correct Christian belief, for instance in determining admission to Christian schools.

[iii] Jesus told his disciples that 'He who has seen me has seen the Father' (John 14: 9). Paul tells the Corinthians that 'God was in Christ, reconciling the world to himself' (2 Corinthians 5:19). John's Gospel states that Christ is the Word of God was made flesh (John 1:14). The Christian experiences God in Christ, forgiveness of sins through Christ, the promise of eternal life through Christ. Paul states that all the fullness of the Godhead dwells in him (Colossians 2:9).

[iv] The Holy Spirit is described both as the 'Spirit of God' and the 'Spirit of Christ' (Romans 8:9). Jesus described it, or he, as 'another Comforter' (John 14:16), whom the Father will send in Jesus' name (John 14:26).

[v] Except for 1 John 5:7 (KJV) 'For there are three that bear record in heaven, the Father, the Word, and the Holy Ghost, and these three are one'. These words are widely acknowledged to be a medieval addition, as they occur in no Greek manuscript until the fourteenth century, except for one manuscript in the eleventh and one in the twelfth century where they have been added in another hand.

[vi] The Council of Constantinople in AD 680 agreed that Christ was one person with two wills, a human will and a divine will.

[vii] Chapter 2 outlines the controversies over whether Christ had two natures or two wills which have led to divisions between East and West to this day.

[viii] Some Messianic Jews (Jews converted to Christianity) claim to find plurality in the nature of God in the Old Testament. See *Three in the Holy One of Israel* by Simon Hawthorne, in *Roots and Branches: Explorations into the Jewish Context of the Christian Faith* (ed. Fieldsend et al). However much of their evidence relies on rabbinic commentaries written after Christ (see later in this chapter).

[ix] The trinitarian view of Deuteronomy 6.4 is that it expresses unity *in agreement* of the supposed three Persons. A non-trinitarian would of course disagree with this.

[x] Some Muslims converted to Christianity see God as plural. See for example Simon Altaf, *Yeshua or Isa.*

[xi] The issue of the Trinity is often entangled with disagreements between Oneness Pentecostals and trinitarians over other matters such as baptism, which have resulted in mutual accusations of not belonging to the true Body of Christ. The John Ankerberg debate (John Ankerberg, 1985) showed the trinitarian representatives accusing the United Pentecostal representatives of saying in their literature that Christians not baptised in the Name of Jesus were not saved.

[xii] Oneness pentecostalism dates from a controversy within the Pentecostal movment in the USA in 1913 over the correct formula for baptism. A 'Oneness' movement was started the following year by F.J. Ewart and G.A. Cook arguing for baptism in the name of Jesus according to Acts 2:38. There are now many oneness pentecostal organisations throughout the world, many of them with parent bodies in the U.S. The largest of these is the United Pentecostal Church International. There are also numerous independent assemblies with such beliefs. Oneness pentecostal theology owes much to Ewart, and his book *The Name and the Book*, first published in 1936. David Bernard in *The Oneness of God* (1983, revised 2000) builds on this foundation to set out a systematic oneness pentecostal theology. There is now a large body of oneness pentecostal writing, and it would be incorrect to describe it as presenting a uniform view.

[xiii] Oneness pentecostalism faces a challenge in accounting for the relationship between the Father and the Son. An obvious question is 'Why does Jesus pray to God, if he is God?' Some oneness pentecostals say that Jesus' prayer was his human nature to his divine nature, and so unlike human prayer, others that it was genuine prayer from a man to his God.

[xiv] There were variant or heretical views about Christ, ranging from the one extreme of adoptionism (Christ being only an anointed man) to the other extreme of docetism (Christ not really human, but an angelic being with only the appearance of humanity). Examples recorded in scripture of the conflict are the explicit attacks on docetism in Colossians 2:9 and 1 John 4:2. The conflict with the varieties of gnostic belief continued until AD 200 or later.

[xv] Between the 2nd and the 4th centuries the Church settled upon the 'canon' of scripture, the 27 books that were to be regarded as authoritative and that we know as the New Testament. There were other documents circulating at the time, such as the Epistles of Clement, the Acts of Paul and the Gospel of Thomas; these were discredited and not included in the canon, mainly because they put forward views which were regarded as heretical, but also because of doubts about 'apostolic' authorship. Marcion drew up his own canon in 140 AD that included only one gospel, an expurgated edition of Luke.

[xvi] Augustine of Hippo, mediaeval scholasticism and the 15th century Renaissance were all influenced by Neoplatonism (see P. Spearritt, Neoplatonism, *A New Dictionary of Christian Theology*, p396).

[xvii] The principal differences between the two trinities are firstly that the Neoplatonic trinity is impersonal whereas each member of the Christian Trinity is a person, and secondly that the second person of the Christian Trinity became a man.

[xviii] Mackey notes the "interchangeability of Word and Spirit" in pre-Nicene binitarian theology, existing "side by side with triadic patterns", *New Dictionary of Christian Theology*, p583.

[xix] Bernard concludes that although Justin identified the Holy Spirit as a third being to worship, he did not distinguish the Spirit clearly from the Father and the Word, nor did he define the relationship between the three. Justin advocated a threefold baptismal formula, which Bernard suggests is the first such recorded instance. (*Oneness and Trinity*, p68).

[xx] The main criterion was *apostolicity*, i.e. being written by an apostle or by the permission of one. Irenaeus defended the Gospel of John as being the work of John son of Zebedee. Applying this criterion led to the exclusion in the west of the Letter to the Hebrews. It was only included in the canon more than 200 years later on the authority of the eastern churches.

[xxi] Tertullian believed that Isaiah 44:24 meant 'the Lord ... that stretcheth forth the heavens alone *with my Son*' (italics his addition), *Against Praxeas* 19.

[xxii] In one place (*de carn. Christi* 13) Tertullian says there are *three* substances, two (soul and flesh) making up his humanity and the third being the Logos. But usually he speaks of two (Mackintosh p156).

[xxiii] Novatian was one of two rival bishops of Rome in a serious division in 250-1. He held the traditional view that the Church had no power to remit sins. His rival Cornelius obtained greater support for his more lenient views.

[xxiv] Tertullian of Carthage was the first theologian to write in Latin (although he knew Greek well). His fellow trinitarian Hippolytus was the last western theologian to write in Greek.

[xxv] Paulinus held that Father, Son and Holy Spirit were the same substance (Greek *hypostasis*). His anti-Arian rival Meletius believed in three *hypostases*. Meletius was eventually given preference (H. Chadwick, p147).

[xxvi] It seems that in the West there was by this time general satisfaction with the subordinationist trinitarian theology of Tertullian and Hippolytus.

[xxvii] However the inclusion of the Spirit in the Godhead as a Third Person was not automatic. J.P. Mackey points out that Basil did not call the Spirit 'God' and Gregory of Nazianzus was reluctant to ascribe equal divine status to a Third Person, *The Christian Experience of God as Trinity*, p150.

[xxviii] This discussion is indebted to J.P. Mackey, *The Christian Experience of God as Trinity*, Chapter 11.

[xxix] The 'cohinerence' (Greek *perichoresis*) of the Persons of the Trinity, according to which each person is involved in each of the other persons, is a doctrine which is found in Irenaeus amd Tertullian, but was developed more fully by Gregory of Nyssa. In modern times the concept has been used by Moltmann in his 'social doctrine' of the Trinity to underpin the unity of God.

[xxx] The creed now known as the Nicene creed, which enlarges on the Holy Spirit as a co-equal member of the Trinity, is not that agreed at Nicaea. Scholars believe that it can be dated to Jerusalem about 370 AD. It came into common use after the Council of Chalcedon in 451 AD.

[xxxi] e.g. Rom 8:9 'the Spirit of Christ'; Gal 4:6 'the Spirit of His Son'; (perhaps) 2 Cor 3:17 'the Spirit of the Lord'; Phil 1:19 'the Spirit of Jesus Christ'.

[xxxii] Mackey summarises the conclusion of Emil Brunner that 'essential' Trinities are not biblical, whereas an 'economic' trinitarian doctrine which respects the strict order of salvation and revelation, the order in which Father, Son and Spirit come after one another, is biblical. E. Brunner, *The Christian Doctrine of God*, 1950, summarised in J.P. Mackey, *New Dictionary*, p581.

[xxxiii] A non-trinitarian alternative to the plural of majesty is to account for these verses in terms of God speaking to the angels. Such an explanation is possible for the last three passages, but Genesis 1:26 requires the plural of majesty for a non-trinitarian explanation.

[xxxiv] The word *elohim* is also used to refer to the false gods (Ps 86:8), angels (Ps 8:5), the mighty (Ps 50:1) or saints.(Ps 82:1, 6).

[xxxv] Psalm 110:1 is quoted by Jesus (Matthew 22:44, Mark 12:36, Luke 20:42) against the Pharisees to show that the Messiah must be more than a descendant of David. However the passages do not show a plurality within the Godhead.

[xxxvi] Simon Altaf, a converted Muslim, takes a similar line in his book *Yeshua or Isa* (p52): 'In the Targums (commentaries on the Bible) … the Memra can take on attributes and a form just like God, and it is the Memra which God uses to create. The Targums state that the Memra is the one to be worshipped, served and obeyed. Else why would God need to say something to God to speak creation (Genesis 1:27) into existence through his Word?' Altaf goes on to cite the Targum Onkelos, a 6th century AD commentary on Genesis 28:20f. In the original verse in the Bible Jacob vows that 'the LORD (YHWH) shall be my God'. In the commentary it is replaced by 'the Word of YHWH shall be my God'.

[xxxvii] God talks of himself in singular terms particularly where he emphasizes monotheism, such as 'I am the Lord and there is none else'. See e.g. Isaiah 42:8, 43:11, 44:6, 44:24, 45:5f, 45:18, 45:22, 46:9, 47:8.

xxxviii Eusebius, Bishop of Caesarea (AD c260 - c340), the historian of the early Church, quotes Matthew 28:19 as "Go ye, and make disciples of all the nations, baptize them in my name". This point is made by Graeser, Lynn and Schoenheit , p332.

xxxix Graeser at al (pp500-504) cite examples of the problems of applying Granville Sharp's rules with certainty to New Testament texts. Some of the reservations cited are made by trinitarian scholars.

xl The language used at Jesus' baptism evokes Psalm 2:7 which describes the adoption of the Israelite king as the 'Son of God' and is usually interpreted as a 'messianic' psalm, looking forward to the adoption of the Messiah as Son of God who will bring God's rule on earth.

xli R. Bowman, The Biblical Basis for the Doctrine of the Trinity, p14.

The texts given are: Luke 1:35, 3:21f, 4:1-12, John 4:10-25, 7:37-39, chaps 14-16, 20:21-22, Acts 1:4-8, 2:33, 2:38f, 5:3f, 5:9, 5:30-32, 7:55f, 10:36-38, 10:44-48, 11:15-18, 15:8-11, Acts 20:38 (perhaps a mistake, perhaps 20:28 is intended), 28:25-31, Romans 1:1-4, 5:5-10, 8:2-4, 8:9-11, 8:14-17, 1 Corinthians 6:11, 12:4-6, 12:11f,18, 2 Corinthians 1:19-22, 3:6-8, 3:14-18, 13:14, Galatians 3:8-14, 4:4-7, Ephesians 1:3-7, 2:18, 2:21-22, 3:14-19, 4:4-6, 4:29-32, 5:18-20, Philippians 3:3, 1 Thessalonians 1:3-6, 2 Thessalonians 2:13f, Titus 3:4-6, Hebrews 2:3f, 9:14, 10:28-31, 1 Peter 1:2, 1 John 3:21-24, 4:13f, Jude 20-21, Revelation 2:18,27-29

xlii God is referred to as 'Father' in a personal sense prophetically on a few occasions, for instance Psalm 89:26. The psalm is a Messianic psalm, and the reference is to the future ideal Davidic king who is able to call on God and say 'Thou art my father, my God and the rock of my salvation'. This sense of the fatherhood of God was not available to the Jews of the Old Testament.

xliii Bowman, in *The Biblical Basis for the Doctrine of the Trinity* (p9), suggests that this verse shows there is a distinction between 'my God' and 'your God', because Jesus never speaks of 'our God'. This is a challenging thesis which Bowman does not seem to substantiate anywhere else.

xliv In James 3:9 the word translated as 'God' is actually the Greek word *kurion* meaning 'Lord'. It is correctly translated as 'Lord' in the NIV, RSV and other translations.

xlv A W Wainwright, in *The Trinity in the New Testament* (pp76f), points out that the Greek word κυριος and derivatives which is translated 'Lord' has four meanings: (a) possessive (as a servant to a master); (b) polite (to convey respect or reverence); (c) courtly (as to a king); and (d) religious (to a god or God).

Jesus is described or referred to as 'Lord' many times in the New Testament. Jesus was undoubtedly addressed as 'Lord' (in the original Aramaic *mari*, meaning 'my Lord') at times in the polite sense by the disciples and others, and this is recorded in the gospels (e.g. John 13:37). However once ascended, he could only be addressed or referred to as 'Lord' meaning master, ruler or as God himself.

[xlvi] It was noted in Chapter 2 that Calvin's theology suggested that the 'economic' Trinity is still needed 'behind the scenes' to support the classical Trinity. The three 'Persons' are supposed to be co-equal, but the Father is in fact the 'first among equals'. In a Trinity where the Son and the Spirit depend on the Father for their being it must be the Father who is the 'real' God and the other two must be subordinate in some way. If they are subordinate but share the same 'being' or 'essence' with the Father, then they are roles or manifestations of the Father. If they are subordinate but different 'beings' then they are gods in their own right and there is more than one god.

[xlvii] This concept of the Trinity resembles more the Eastern model than the Western model, with the Father recognised as the source of the other two Persons (see Chapter 2).

[xlviii] It is debatable whether the famous sayings of Jesus recorded in John 8:58 ('Before Abraham was, I am') and 10:30 ('I and the Father are one') show him speaking as God in the sense of showing a divine self-consciousness. For, in both cases, the immediate context shows Jesus talking about 'my Father' (8:54f, 10:25-29, 32, 36-38), who is clearly other than Jesus, and must refer to God himself not a First Person (see Chapter 4). Jesus speaks of 'the Father' as the one who is honouring Jesus and authenticating his ministry. This would make no sense if Jesus were speaking with the voice of God.

[xlix] Psalm 2 is recognised by scholars as a so-called 'royal psalm' celebrating the enthronement of the king of Israel (see verse 6) and his recognition as God's adopted son. However it is also regarded as a so-called 'messianic psalm' speaking prophetically of Jesus (see for instance Acts 13:33, where Paul specifically applies it to Jesus).

[l] J. Pelikan, the historian of Christian doctrine, in The *Christian Tradition*, p189, notes that in the original usage in the New Testament the title 'Son of God' referred to the historical person of Jesus, not to a preexistent being. For instance in Colossians 1:13, Paul uses the term 'his Son'. This means the Son of 'the Father' referred to in the previous verse. Because 'the Father' is God Himself, not a 'God the Father' of a Trinity, then 'the Son' must refer to the Son of God not a 'God the Son' of a Trinity. A similar use of 'the Son' is recorded in Hebrews 1, where 'Son' (verse 2) is the Son of God (verse 1).

[li] Bowman, in *The Biblical Basis for the Doctrine of the Trinity* (p9), appears to suggest that in John 20:17 there is a distinction between 'my God' and 'your God', because Jesus never speaks of 'our God'. However this is quite weak evidence for the belief that Jesus is talking about a different being or person when he talks to his Father as when he tells his disciples to talk to their 'Father in heaven'. Bowman does not seem to substantiate this argument anywhere else.

[lii] The Old Testament context of Psalm 2 would almost certainly be the coronation of the king of Israel. In Old Testament thought, the king was seen as the adopted son of God.

[liii] 'The Father' is used only in John 1:14, where it clearly means God, not a 'God the Father'. The Evangelist talks of God as 'the Father'.

[liv] Other interpretations suggested are 'God is your throne ...', 'Your throne is a throne of God ...' and 'God has enthroned you ...'. The last suggestion is from Dahood, *Psalms*, Doubleday, 1965.

[lv] Revelation Chapters 4 and 5 describes the scene in heaven. There is the throne and he who is seated on the throne (5:1). There is the Lamb standing between the throne and the four living creatures (5:6). But where is the Spirit? The most that can be said about the Spirit is that John was 'in the Spirit' (4:2), and that before the throne were seven torches 'which are the seven spirits of God' (4:5). If God were a Trinity, we would surely expect to see more of the Third Person in this scene.

[lvi] A trinitarian may make the point that omission of the Spirit from Genesis 1:1-3 does not prove non-existence, i.e. that just because the Spirit is not mentioned in John 1:1-3 does not prove that it was not there as a Third Person. However trinitarians place a lot of weight upon Genesis 1:1-3 because the Spirit of God *is* mentioned. The absence of the Spirit from John 1:1-3 shows it to be a poor witness for the Trinity - but this is never mentioned in trinitarian arguments.

[lvii] As examples of how trinitarian views come close to tritheism when trinitarians and non-trinitarians debate using the Bible, see two recent debates between David Bernard representing the oneness view and trinitarian scholars. The first, Dr Eugene Carpenter, talked about 'separate beings' when citing evidence from Daniel 7, and the second, Dr Robert Morey used the analogy of the Trinity with three separate individuals sharing the same human nature. The debate with Dr Morey referred to Dr Morey's description in a previous debate of the Trinity as analogous to three men sharing the same human nature (debates between Dr David Bernard and Dr Eugene Carpenter representing the Trinity, February, 2005, and between Dr David Bernard and Dr Robert Morey, St Louis AM630 radio, July 6 2001, audiocassettes, Word Aflame Press, Hazelwood, 2005).

[lviii] To illustrate the variety of views on how many 'Persons' can be experienced, a trinitarian friend of the author reported that she *can* identify the separate voices of the persons of the Trinity. Yet this appears to contradict the principle of *opera ad extra sunt indivisa* which states that the works of the Trinity, seen from outside, are indivisable. This would imply that the voices of the persons *cannot* be distinguished. The Bible does not seem to give answers to these kind of questions.